New Directions for
Higher Education

Martin Kramer
EDITOR-IN-CHIEF

International Policy Perspectives on Improving Learning with Limited Resources

Carolin Kreber
EDITOR

Number 133 • Spring 2006
Jossey-Bass
San Francisco

INTERNATIONAL POLICY PERSPECTIVES ON IMPROVING LEARNING WITH
LIMITED RESOURCES
Carolin Kreber (ed.)
New Directions for Higher Education, no. 133
Martin Kramer, Editor-in-Chief

Microfilm copies of issues and articles are available in 16mm and 35mm,
as well as microfiche in 105mm, through University Microfilms Inc., 300
North Zeeb Road, Ann Arbor, Michigan 48106-1346.

NEW DIRECTIONS FOR HIGHER EDUCATION (ISSN 0271-0560, electronic ISSN
1536-0741) is part of The Jossey-Bass Higher and Adult Education Series
and is published quarterly by Wiley Subscription Services, Inc., A Wiley
Company, at Jossey-Bass, 989 Market Street, San Francisco, California
94103-1741. Periodicals Postage Paid at San Francisco, California, and at
additional mailing offices. POSTMASTER: Send address changes to New
Directions for Higher Education, Jossey-Bass, 989 Market Street, San
Francisco, California 94103-1741.

New Directions for Higher Education is indexed in Current Index to Journals in Education (ERIC); Higher Education Abstracts.

SUBSCRIPTIONS cost $80 for individuals and $180 for institutions, agencies,
and libraries. See ordering information page at end of journal.

EDITORIAL CORRESPONDENCE should be sent to the Editor-in-Chief,
Martin Kramer, 2807 Shasta Road, Berkeley, California 94708-2011.

Cover photograph © Digital Vision

www.josseybass.com

CONTENTS

EDITOR'S NOTES

This volume brings together a group of higher education specialists from nine countries to discuss the policy perspectives taken within their respective jurisdictions with reference to higher education—in particular, policies aimed at enhancing the quality of university teaching and learning. Contributions were invited from Europe (Finland, Germany, Belgium, and the United Kingdom), Australia, Brazil, the United States, Canada, and South Africa. The contributors to this volume are senior scholars of higher education as a field of study. Having a deep understanding of the higher education context within their own countries, they are exceptionally well prepared to comment on present approaches and future developments on the national scene.

The main challenge with this volume was to find scholars of higher education who are also aware of, though not necessarily directly involved in, the field of educational development in higher education. In most instances this challenge was met successfully in that the choice of contributors was perfect. On two occasions, once chapter drafts were submitted it appeared that, although the authors were clearly aware of the policy context within which higher education systems in their countries operate, the potential influences of this general policy context on policy and practices with respect to educational development were left somewhat underexplored. It seems plausible to conclude that such initiatives likely play a less prominent role in these countries, at least at the level of national policy, but as is noted in these chapters, local schemes operating on a smaller scale are in place at individual higher education institutions.

Each contributor was asked to attempt a critical analysis of the effectiveness and appropriateness of present policy perspectives within his or her country and, if applicable, to make suggestions for how remaining challenges could be addressed. Though some authors tackled the task through the lens of a specific institution in their country, the book is not in essence a compilation of institutional case studies. Instead, it is a series of national case studies in which illustrations of how national policy was put into practice in specific institutions were incorporated as was deemed suitable by the individual authors. Such concrete examples of how specific institutions put certain policies into operation were very welcome because they contributed considerably to readability. The main purpose of this volume is to highlight national differences in development and implementation of higher education policy with regard to university teaching and learning. Identifying how these policies may influence individual universities in their institutional approaches to enhancement of teaching and learning was then the second goal.

NEW DIRECTIONS FOR HIGHER EDUCATION, no. 133, Spring 2006 © Wiley Periodicals, Inc.
Published online in Wiley InterScience (www.interscience.wiley.com) • DOI: 10.1002/he.199

Most important, the volume documents the approaches that a number of countries have taken to enhancing teaching and learning during a period that is generally recognized as one of drastic and rapid change, resource constraints, and increased performance accountability.

In Chapter Two, Gene Rice provides an overview of the situation in the United States and concludes by inviting readers to reflect on whether traditional understanding of the faculty member who both teaches and is involved in research is still sustainable in this era of mass education. In Chapter Three, Janet Gail Donald describes developments in university teaching for the Canadian context over the past thirty years. Despite much public rhetoric directed at the importance of university teaching and learning, Donald takes a rather skeptical view as to the extent to which adequate policies aimed at enhancement of student learning have been developed in that country, taking particular issue with the low level of funding available for the study of student learning.

In Chapter Four, John Dearn documents the situation for Australia, which in many ways shares features with what can be observed within the UK context. Brenda Smith, in Chapter Five, describes a nationwide policy agenda in the United Kingdom to professionalize university teaching and the various initiatives introduced over the past decade to attain this goal. In Chapter Six, Wolff-Dietrich Webler offers an overview of developments aimed at enhancing the quality of university teaching in Germany, referring (as do all four European contributors) to the impact of the Bologna Process (a policy initiative in Europe aimed, among other things, at reaching greater compatibility of degrees across institutions in Europe and beyond).

In Chapters Seven and Eight, Sari Lindblom-Ylänne and Piet Verhesschen give an overview of national policy initiatives in each of their countries and then focus on how these policies were implemented institutionally. Lindblom-Ylänne describes initiatives taken at the University of Helsinki in Finland, and Verhesschen illustrates initiatives at the Katholieke Universiteit Leuven in Flanders (Belgium). In Chapter Nine, Philip Higgs and Berte van Wyk offer an overview of the general higher education context in South Africa but take a very different approach to the questions. Tackling the subject from a philosophical angle, they discuss their views on the values and assumptions that ought to guide higher education in post-apartheid South Africa and some of the implications for policy development this might entail. In Chapter Ten, José Dias Sobrinho shows the drastic changes Brazil has experienced in its higher education policies over the past ten years and identifies some challenges that remain.

Carolin Kreber
Editor

CAROLIN KREBER is director of the Centre for Teaching, Learning, and Assessment at the University of Edinburgh, Scotland, where she is also professor of teaching and learning in higher education in the department of higher and community education.

1

Growing student access and factors associated with globalization affect higher education's organization, purpose, and delivery.

Setting the Context: The Climate of University Teaching and Learning

Carolin Kreber

In this first chapter, I provide an overall assessment of the present higher education environment within which university teaching and learning take place. Because several excellent and comprehensive analyses of the various political, economic, and social influences on the current higher education context exist elsewhere (Altbach, Berdahl, and Gumport, 1999; Enders and Fulton, 2002; Jones, McCarney, and Skolnik, 2005; Trow, 2000), my remarks in this volume are limited to a few essential observations.

General Context of Higher Education

It is widely documented that the process of *economic globalization* has resulted in new demands on education in terms of knowledge and educated labor. Ensuring the "employability" of graduates, for example, has been identified as an important graduate outcome in many countries (Department for Education and Skills, 2003; Yorke and Knight, 2003; Teichler, 1999; WCHE, 1998). Perhaps not surprisingly, there is considerable agreement across countries on the qualifications university students should have to graduate. Among them are that students should:

- Be able and willing to contribute to innovation and be creative
- Be able to cope with uncertainties
- Be interested in and prepared for life-long learning

NEW DIRECTIONS FOR HIGHER EDUCATION, no. 133, Spring 2006 © Wiley Periodicals, Inc.
Published online in Wiley InterScience (www.interscience.wiley.com) • DOI: 10.1002/he.200

- Have acquired social sensitivity and communicative skills
- Be able to work in teams
- Be willing to take on responsibilities
- Become entrepreneurial
- Prepare themselves for the internationalization of the labor market through an understanding of various cultures
- Be versatile in generic skills that cut across disciplines
- Be literate in areas of knowledge forming the basis for various professional skills, for example, in new technologies (WCHE, 1998)

These same qualifications are noted by those who believe that higher education institutions should prepare students for lifelong learning (Knapper and Cropley, 2001). It also has been argued that the skills, abilities, and personal qualities typically associated with employability are critical not only for being successful in the work setting but also for contributing effectively in other social environments (Yorke and Knight, 2003).

There is wide agreement that these learning outcomes pose considerable challenges for higher education institutions as more and more students enter higher education. Among the questions that require thoughtful debate: How can institutions strike a balance between skills development on the one hand and knowledge acquisition on the other? How can specialized training and development be complemented with more generic education and training? Are our faculty adequately prepared for these more complex roles?

It is generally acknowledged that rising pressure to remain competitive in the research arena, in addition to teaching a steadily increasing and diverse student population in times of declining resources, place new demands on our faculty (Evans, Forney, and Guido-DiBrito, 1998; Martin and Ramsden, 2000). Some observers also argue that many students today are less well prepared than in the past (for example, Aronowitz, 2000), more vocationally oriented (Stark and Lattuca, 1997), and less politically engaged (Ehrlich, 2001). Others comment that today's undergraduate students are more culturally diverse, that many study in a foreign language, and that they tend to be older and pursue their education part-time because of family and job responsibilities (Cranton, 1998). Indeed, as one study observed, "fewer students in postsecondary programs actually define themselves as students" (Donald, 1997, p. 85).

Although the general context in which university teaching and learning take place has become increasingly complex, the pressures on academic staff to publish (particularly at research-intensive institutions) have never been greater as institutions are called on to demonstrate the "usefulness" of their research. There is also a widely shared observation that, internationally, universities have become progressively more corporate as they begin to model their internal governance structures after big organizations that emphasize efficiency and effectiveness, and more profit-driven (Aronowitz, 2000; Newson and Buchbinder, 1988; Slaughter, 1998; Fisher and Rubenson,

1998). A (new) managerialism is developing and becoming entrenched in the academy, and some critics caution that universities could far too easily lose sight of such traditional values as curiosity-driven research, social criticism, and preparation for civic life. As Paul Axelrod (2002) observes for the Canadian context: "More than ever, higher education is expected to cater directly, quickly, and continually to the demands of the marketplace. . . . Preparing graduates for employment is undeniably part of the university endeavour . . . but in the race for riches, symbolized by endless rhetoric about the need for Canada to become globally competitive, technologically advanced, and proficient at churning out 'knowledge workers' for the twenty-first century, something significant is being lost" (pp. 3–4).

As higher education institutions experience declining government funding, they face growing pressure to demonstrate their legitimacy and purpose. Although internationally participation in higher education has widened as a result of national policies ensuring greater access, higher education institutions today compete within a common global market for staff, students, graduates, and alternative sources of income (Kivinen, 2002). Institutions therefore engage in a variety of efforts to increase their revenue. Active recruiting of foreign students who pay higher (differential) fees, wider access to part-time students, and marketing of special programs are commonly used strategies. An increasing number of private institutions offering career-specific degrees present a serious challenge, particularly when they are large, like the University of Phoenix in Arizona, and extremely successful in attracting an ever growing number of working adults from all over the world by "guaranteeing" that their degrees are relevant to real life and can be obtained online in two or three years (University of Phoenix, 2005).

Given cutbacks in government funding, institutions also tend to establish partnerships with business and industry, which in turn can have direct implications with regard to their programs, curricula, and research agendas.

It is evident that institutions experience growing pressure to demonstrate their effectiveness in both research and teaching. Quality assurance agencies, which come under different names and serve to strengthen external control of teaching quality—specifically but not exclusively the quality of degrees conferred—have been launched through government initiative in many jurisdictions; the Bologna Process, for example (for details, see also Chapters Six, Seven, and Eight) is among other goals intended to standardize the quality assurance of higher education systems throughout Europe. Certainly this is of interest also to non-European countries at a time when public funds are scarce and universities compete in an international market for students and revenue. Public reports on quality will likely enter into the decision-making processes of those our universities hope to serve. How quality is interpreted, and by extension how it is assessed, as well as the implications of greater control with respect to institutional autonomy, are critical issues to consider.

Purpose and Organization of this Volume

Against this general background, this volume explores whether (and if so, how) these global trends toward greater performance accountability in terms of teaching as well as research are reflected in national policies geared directly at teaching and learning in higher education institutions. Specifically, do these policies tend to lead approaches universities themselves have taken with the goal of supporting and enhancing teaching and learning within their specific contexts, and if so, how? The relationships are not necessarily straightforward; however, the general context within which higher education takes place nationally as well as internationally needs to be considered in present and future discussions about university teaching and learning. This is the case largely because the extent to which institutions are prepared to invest in teaching and learning is likely associated with (though surely not exclusively a function of) the general pressures they experience with regard to performance accountability in teaching and research. Educational developers, vice principals, and others directly charged with enhancing learning and teaching locally need to be aware of this larger context and understand the at-times messy relationship between external pressure and an institution's (and its faculty's) motivation to enhance pedagogy. In the end, educational developers face the same issue as the institutions themselves in that they will have to demonstrate their value. It might be helpful to draw a distinction between "legitimacy" and "value." In times of increased external performance evaluation and accountability, educational development assumes almost an inherent legitimacy. More and more, institutions create services or units charged specifically with the support of learning and teaching because not doing so would be politically disadvantageous. In other words, institutions can no longer afford to be perceived externally as "not caring" about learning and teaching. However, the real value that institutions and their faculty attribute to the role of these units is directly linked to whether or not the units, and more important the people within and the work done by them, are perceived to fit the institution's larger strategic plan, which of course in and of itself is linked to how institutions have decided to respond to the challenges posed by the current higher education context.

In an attempt to explore the multiple links between external higher education policy context and supports for teaching and learning, each contributor was asked to address a number of points, though not necessarily separately or in the order they appear here. Some of the points also make more sense within the context of certain countries than in others.

- Provide some background to the higher education system in their country (for example, number of higher education institutions, or HEI, and number of universities among them; participation rates; governance; funding; degree of autonomy; and so on).

NEW DIRECTIONS FOR HIGHER EDUCATION • DOI 10.1002/he

- Describe how the quality of teaching and learning at universities is controlled or supported (for instance, quality assurance agencies).
- Describe whether the quality of teaching and learning is linked to funding for institutions, and if so, how.
- Comment on any important policy documents that have been issued in their country and on the impact they had on approaches aimed at enhancing teaching and learning (what did these policy documents suggest?).
- If applicable, discuss if funding is available for academic staff in their country to engage in inquiry on teaching and learning or professional development projects.
- Discuss any associations or initiatives in their country that are directly aimed at enhancing university teaching and learning.
- Identify the critical issues that still need to be addressed in their country to enhance teaching and learning in universities. What are the chief challenges?
- Comment on important recent developments with regard to teaching and learning policies at universities in their country.
- Highlight the differences, if any, between support for teaching and learning at universities and other higher education institutions in their country or nation-state, particularly with regard to institutional strategies.
- If applicable, describe specifically what has been done to enhance research and teaching links (at the undergraduate level).
- If applicable, comment on possible tensions between research and teaching requirements generally, and in view of recent developments specifically.
- Comment on how successful past and recent policy and institutional initiatives aimed at enhancing university teaching and learning have been (attempt a critical analysis, comment on remaining challenges, and make suggestions for how they could be overcome).

The contributors tackled these challenging questions in unique ways and according to how relevant they perceived them to be with respect to their national context. Not all contributors addressed all twelve questions, and there was no expectation they would. Generally, most found it difficult to respond to the questions within the allotted space of thirty-five hundred words, but all succeeded in furnishing an interesting overview of the situation within their country. It is probably also fair to say that in the end not all felt sufficiently qualified to offer an answer to some of these complex questions and avoided them for that reason. Given the varying degree to which contributors chose to engage with the questions, the final chapter posed somewhat of a challenge because it was envisaged as a comparative analysis of the contexts and approaches described in each country with the goal of highlighting issues common to all countries and those particular to some. The last chapter nevertheless concludes with an attempt at identifying what can be learned from the successes and challenges that were reported.

NEW DIRECTIONS FOR HIGHER EDUCATION • DOI 10.1002/he

The intent of the volume is to offer much-needed documentation of policy approaches taken in a number countries but also an analysis of why certain approaches are more effective than others, why some fail, or perhaps most important why some are effective and feasible in one country but not in another. The volume thus seeks to highlight the context specificity of attempts to enhance university teaching and learning at the level of national, state, or local policy. This volume may not reach its goal entirely, but it lays the groundwork for future projects in this area.

References

Altbach, P. G., Berdahl, R. O., and Gumport, P. J. (eds.). *American Higher Education in the Twenty-First Century: Social, Political, and Economic Challenges.* Baltimore: Johns Hopkins University Press, 1999.

Aronowitz, S. *The Knowledge Factory: Dismantling the Corporate University and Creating True Higher Learning.* Boston: Beacon Press, 2000.

Axelrod, P. D. *Values in Conflict: The University, the Marketplace and the Trials of Liberal Education.* Montreal: McGill-Queen's University Press, 2002.

Cranton, P. A. *No One Way.* Toronto: Wall and Emerson, 1998.

Department for Education and Skills. "The Future of Higher Education" (white paper). Norwich, UK: Department for Education and Skills, 2003.

Donald, J. G. *Improving the Environment for Learning.* San Francisco: Jossey-Bass, 1997.

Ehrlich, T. "Education for Responsible Citizenship: A Challenge for Faculty Developers." In D. Lieberman and C. Wehlburg (eds.), *To Improve the Academy: Resources for Faculty, Instructional, and Organizational Development.* Bolton, Mass.: Anker, 2001.

Enders, J., and Fulton, O. (eds.). *Higher Education in a Globalizing World: International Trends and Mutual Observations.* A Festschrift in Honour of Ulrich Teichler. Dordrecht, Neth.: Kluwer Academic, 2002.

Evans, N. J., Forney, D. S., and Guido-DiBrito, F. *Student Development in College: Theory, Research, and Practice.* San Francisco: Jossey-Bass, 1998.

Fisher, D., and Rubenson, K. "The Changing Political Economy: The Private and Public Lives of Canadian Universities." In J. Currie and J. Newson (eds.), *Universities and Globalization: Critical Perspectives.* Thousand Oaks, Calif.: Sage, 1998.

Jones, G. A., McCarney, P. L., and Skolnik, M. L. *Creating Knowledge, Strengthening Nations: The Changing Role of Higher Education.* Toronto: University of Toronto Press, 2005.

Kivinen, O. "Higher Education in an Age of Uncertainty: From Postmodern Critique to Appropriate University Practices." In J. Enders and O. Fulton (eds.), *Higher Education in a Globalizing World: International Trends and Mutual Observations. A Festschrift in Honour of Ulrich Teichler.* Dordrecht, Neth.: Kluwer Academic, 2002.

Knapper, C., and Cropley, A. *Lifelong Learning in Higher Education* (3rd ed.). London: Kogan Page, 2001.

Martin, E., and Ramsden, P. "Introduction." *Higher Education Research and Development,* 2000, *19*(2), 133–135.

Newson, J., and Buchbinder, H. *The University Means Business: Universities, Corporations and Academic Work.* Toronto: Garamond Press, 1988.

Slaughter, S. "National Higher Education Policies in a Global Economy." In J. Currie and J. Newson (eds.), *Universities and Globalization: Critical Perspectives.* Thousand Oaks, Calif.: Sage, 1998.

Stark, J., and Lattuca, L. R. *Reshaping the College Curriculum: Academic Plans in Action.* Boston: Allyn and Bacon, 1997.

Teichler, U. "Higher Education Policy and the World of Work: Changing Conditions and Challenges." *Higher Education Policy,* 1999, *12,* 285–312.

Trow, M. "From Mass Education to Universal Access: The American Advantage." Research and Occasional Paper Series 1.00. Berkeley: Center for Studies in Higher Education (CSHE), University of California, 2000.

University of Phoenix. 2005. http://www.phoenix.edu/about_us/.

World Conference on Higher Education (WCHE). *Higher Education in the Twenty-First Century: Vision and Action.* Vol. I, Final Report. Paris: UNESCO, 1998.

Yorke, M., and Knight, P. *The Undergraduate Curriculum and Employability.* York, U.K.: Enhancing Student Employability Co-ordinaton Team (ESECT) and Learning and Teaching Support Network (LTSN) Generic Centre, 2003.

CAROLIN KREBER is director of the Centre for Teaching, Learning, and Assessment at the University of Edinburgh, where she is also professor of teaching and learning in higher education in the Department of Higher and Community Education.

2

*In the United States greater attention is being paid to
learning that is more collaborative, actively engaged, and
technologically enhanced.*

Enhancing the Quality of Teaching and Learning: The U.S. Experience

R. Eugene Rice

In recent rankings of the world's two hundred best universities, the *London Times Higher Education Supplement* found the top three to be U.S. institutions: Harvard, University of California Berkeley, and Massachusetts Institute of Technology. In reflecting on the factors contributing to this achievement, Charles Vest, president of MIT, identified several structural and policy elements leading to selection of these research universities that I am confident contribute to the quality of university teaching as well.

The Diversity of Institutions

To my surprise, the first key element identified by President Vest was the diversity of the two hundred institutions. Students and faculty can choose from a variety of colleges and universities—public and private, large and small, faith-based and essentially secular. This rich mosaic of colleges and universities includes historically black institutions and those where the majority of the students are Hispanic, women's and men's colleges, and specialized institutions and colleges with a central commitment to liberal education. There is recognition—explicit or not—that there is a connection among personal identity, choice, and the quality of learning. Over the last twenty years, higher education in the United States has made a shift of significant proportions; the focus is now less on teaching and more on learning. The diversity of institutions—and the democratic press for equity and access that led to this

NEW DIRECTIONS FOR HIGHER EDUCATION, no. 133, Spring 2006 © Wiley Periodicals, Inc.
Published online in Wiley InterScience (www.interscience.wiley.com) • DOI: 10.1002/he.201

development—has cultivated this primary concern with the learner and the value of what is learned.

The diversity of institutions opens the way for introducing innovations in teaching and learning that can be replicated across sectors of U.S. higher education. The best examples are new pedagogical advances originating in two-year community colleges, where the focus is primarily on teaching and learning. These then move up through the larger system and have an instructional impact even on research-intensive universities. Another example is the role of small experimental colleges in the private sector; because of size and independence, they can launch entirely new programs and test their viability. Many of the innovations that now enhance the quality of instruction across higher education in the United States began in these settings.

The history of the diversification process in higher education in the United States, beginning with the nine colleges of the English colonies and extending to the approximately four thousand postsecondary institutions in place now, is a fascinating one. The new republic turned to colleges to cultivate the next generation of democratic leaders, and as the country expanded westward, religious communities founded most of the small, residential liberal arts colleges that proliferated across nineteenth-century America. Here teaching had an honored place, although shaping the moral character of students often held priority. By the beginning of the twentieth century, the new American research universities patterned after the German ideals of *Wissenschaft* (value-free inquiry and advancement of knowledge for its own sake) had taken root; the perpetual struggle between teaching and research was launched. Research universities included by intention and policy a commitment to providing instruction for undergraduate students.

The diversity of U.S. universities and colleges was enriched by the introduction of land-grant institutions with the passage of the Morrill Land-Grant Acts of 1862 and 1890. The purpose of these schools was to address the agricultural and industrial needs of a developing nation. They include such large state universities as Michigan State, University of California Davis, and Colorado State. Engagement with the larger community not only strengthened the applied research agenda but shaped the pedagogical thrust of this sector of state institutions. In large rural areas, county agencies were established to assist farmers in making the most of technological innovations in agriculture. "Outreach," as it was called, became an academic priority with its own instructional processes; much of this instruction is now computer-based. Growing out of this pedagogical concern with outreach and community engagement is a contemporary movement having a major impact on instruction across all sectors of American higher education; it is growing under the rubric of "service learning." This pedagogical emphasis builds on what is being learned from research on the effectiveness of active learning.

Beginning in the latter part of the nineteenth century, the private sector made a major effort to democratize American higher education. Colleges and universities were established to make a place for people who had earlier been denied access to advanced learning. Women, African Americans, Native Americans, Catholics, Jews, the economically disenfranchised, and other excluded groups either began their own institutions or made sources of support available to build institutions that greatly enhanced the diversity of U.S. colleges and universities. The connection between diversity and the quality of what is learned is now a matter of debate in the U.S. Supreme Court.

Following World War II, the United States entered an era of mass education. The rapid growth of the student population by 1980 to twelve million students forced states to greatly expand the number of public colleges and universities. Now, more than 80 percent of U.S. students are educated in state schools, with large comprehensive universities and community (two-year) colleges absorbing most of that growth. This demographic press—in terms of numbers, diversity, and variation in level of preparation—ratcheted up the need for American higher education to attend to the quality of teaching and learning. Older assumptions about teaching were aggressively challenged on campus and on public and private governing boards. Throughout American society, higher education is now seen as the key to success in a knowledge-based economy. Expectations surrounding the quality of teaching and learning have been dramatically elevated.

Academic Freedom and Institutional Independence

The second factor the president of MIT identified as contributing most to excellence and competitive success in U.S. higher education is academic freedom. He writes, "New assistant professors have freedom to choose what they teach as well as research." I would expand that to say colleges and universities have had relative independence from pressures of the state, church, or business communities in charting their academic pursuits.

Although the concept of academic freedom is uniquely American, the origins of the notion can be traced to the nineteenth century and German professors' claim of *Lernfreiheit* (freedom to learn) and *Lehrfreiheit* (freedom of inquiry). American faculty often cite Max Weber's dictum, "The moral obligation of the teacher is to ask inconvenient questions" (Gerth and Mills, 1946, p. 147). Academic freedom in the United States is linked to broader democratic commitments to civil liberties, free speech, and wide access to information. The 1940 "Statement of Principles on Academic Freedom and Tenure" issued jointly by two voluntary associations—the American Association of University Professors and the Association of American Colleges—assures faculty of their rights and responsibilities related to teaching their subject matter, engaging in research, and serving the larger population without interference from their own institutions, government entities, or citizens.

In the 1950s, the U.S. House of Representatives' "Un-American Activities Committee" sought to identify communist sympathizers. Faculty members across the country were targeted, and the academic freedom of the teaching faculty was seriously challenged. In a 1957 Supreme Court decision, Justice Felix Frankfurter established the faculty's "four essential freedoms": the right "to determine for itself on academic grounds who may teach, what may be taught, how it shall be taught, and who may be admitted to study" (*Sweezy v. New Hampshire*, p. 263).

In the American college and university, teaching was grounded in a collegial culture that assumed quality would be maintained through peer review and faculty and the institutions themselves would monitor whether appropriate standards were being maintained. Quality assurance was largely an internal responsibility. In 1968, Jenks and Riesman published *The Academic Revolution*, declaring that the faculty had become central to the mission and purpose of the American college or university.

Beginning in the 1970s, a managerial culture started to grow in strength and challenge the kind of independence and control that was earlier assumed. Managing the rapidly expanding and complex institutions that were developing required a different kind of organizational expertise, and new productivity standards were invoked.

Financial restraints necessitating greater efficiency in teaching and learning surfaced across the states. "Doing more with less" became a slogan that began shaping delivery of instruction, particularly in large comprehensive universities and community colleges.

The freedom that had earlier shaped the conception of the role of the professor began to be challenged fundamentally. The increasing importance of instructional technology and the emergence of new and effective for-profit universities led to a call for "unbundling" the faculty role. This represented a serious challenge to the more holistic conception of the teacher/scholar rooted in a collegial culture where peer review and self-monitoring were the norm. Along with the collegial culture—and the academic freedom it assumed—went an institutional independence that had been a hallmark of U.S. higher education for so long, though taken for granted. This culture and independence are now being challenged by a new era of assessment and accountability. The tension between the collegial culture and the managerial could hardly be greater; it is having a large impact on teaching and how it is organized in the American college and university.

Accountability, Accreditation, and Assessment

Individual and institutional independence have played key roles in maintaining the creativity, drive for improvement, and attraction to teaching in U.S. colleges and universities. Early on, the dependence of private institutions on support from churches and other donors as well as income generated by student tuition produced its own external accountability. In the 1960s and early 1970s, the quality of teaching and faculty vitality were sustained by institutional growth, staff turnover, and faculty with new ideas, innovative approaches, and often freshly minted Ph.D.s.

In 1974, a small booklet titled "Professional Development in a Time of Retrenchment" was widely distributed, documenting the changing climate in U.S. colleges and universities. No longer could the vitality of faculty and institutions depend on institutional expansion and faculty mobility. Earlier assumptions about growth and generation of additional resources no longer had currency. New strategies for supporting the development of faculty and the quality of teaching were required. The call for accountability was beginning to be heard.

The demand for external accountability grew throughout the 1980s and the 1990s as escalating costs and competition for diminishing resources drew wider public attention to issues of effectiveness and productivity. States began to mandate documentation of student achievement outcomes, measures of faculty workload, and benchmarks related directly to public policy agendas such as the press for greater diversity, better access, and quality performance (Altbach, Berdahl, and Gumport, 1999).

In contrast to many other countries where accreditation and quality assurance are carried out by government, accreditation in the United States is conducted by private nonprofit organizations designed for that specific purpose. The accreditation structure is—like U.S. higher education itself—decentralized. Six regional associations, established in the late nineteenth and early twentieth centuries, work with common accreditation criteria and require colleges and universities to periodically submit to a peer-reviewed quality assurance process. When the broad concern for accountability emerged in the 1980s, the accreditation process began to shift from a focus on existing resources and capacity building—inputs, if you will—to assessment of student learning outcomes. This development marked a major change in the accreditation process and focused the process on whether or not teaching makes a difference.

The focus on student learning outcomes was accompanied by another significant change. Following the lead of U.S. business and industry, accreditation agencies began to call for "continuous quality improvement." In the words of Russell Edgerton, the old American adage "if it ain't broke don't fix it" gave way to a new philosophy of the need for continuous improvement. The regional accrediting agencies, with the assistance of the Pew Charitable Trusts and the Carnegie Foundation for the Advancement of Teaching, are now struggling to develop an assessment process that will lead to "evidence-based practice." One example of a process that leads in this direction is the "institutional portfolio."

Working hand-in-hand with these developments in accreditation is the national assessment movement, which after twenty years has reached agreement that improving student learning is its primary goal. Increasing attention is being paid to what faculty do in the classroom and in other settings in which students learn. In 1992, the Assessment Forum, sponsored by the American Association for Higher Education, produced the document *Principles of Good Practice for Assessing Student Learning,* which received widespread attention. National reports and policy statements calling for improvement of teaching effectiveness and institutional accountability for the quality of student learning are appearing with greater frequency. Attempts to measure the quality of teaching and learning are forcing a national debate over the structure of faculty work and the relationship to others on campus who contribute to student learning.

Recent Initiatives to Enhance Teaching and Learning

As we have seen, concern for the quality of teaching and learning in U.S. colleges and universities escalated dramatically after the mid-1970s. Since then, there have been a range of vibrant and energetic responses. Large private foundations were among the first to launch major initiatives. Kellogg, Lilly, Danforth, Ford, and a number of other national foundations known for supporting education responded. Consortia of liberal arts colleges were among the first to receive these competitive grants. The Fund for the Improvement of Post-Secondary Education, located in the U.S. Department of Education, took up the challenge and funded a number of especially creative initiatives (although the amount of support was relatively modest).

Many of the new endeavors focused on professional development of faculty. Those providing leadership for this initiative formed a national organization, the Professional and Organizational Development Network in Higher Education (POD). A number of us involved in starting this initiative feared the organization was a short-term fad that would disappear after the initial spurt of enthusiasm passed. This did not happen; POD grew rapidly and has evolved into a major professional association committed to the improvement of teaching. Centers for Teaching and Learning, Excellence in Teaching, and Faculty Development—or others known by a variety of names—have been established on most college and university campuses in the United States, funded by the institutions themselves. Early on, leadership and participation in POD were drawn from smaller, private institutions with a focus on faculty and how their effectiveness in teaching could be sustained. Later, the center of gravity shifted to larger research universities with responsibility for maintaining a sizable cohort of teaching assistants responsible for a major part of the institution's undergraduate instruction. Where discipline-based faculty with special interests and talent in teaching were more inclined to get involved in the early years—and then move on to more prestigious academic positions or back to the classroom—the leadership positions in programs for teaching and learning soon became an established career path in U.S. higher education.

NEW DIRECTIONS FOR HIGHER EDUCATION • DOI 10.1002/he

The interest in faculty development and teaching improvement has been greatly enhanced in the United States by a significant demographic shift. The opening of the twenty-first century has brought with it a major generational change in the teaching staffs of colleges and universities. Faculty appointed during what is referred to as the "golden age" of U.S. higher education—the expansionist period of growth in the 1960s—are now retiring in large numbers. New instructional staff are being regularly introduced. They are older, more diverse, and more female, and the majority of the full-time faculty appointed since 1990 are not on a tenure track. Finkelstein and Schuster speak of a "silent revolution" taking place (Rice, 2005). This is both an enormous opportunity and a difficult challenge. Because of these demographic changes, teaching and learning in the American college and university will never be the same.

In 1990, the Association of American Colleges and Universities and the Council of Graduate Schools initiated a foundation-funded Preparing Future Faculty program. It worked with graduate students interested in becoming professors. A special effort was made to link these students to teaching opportunities in other sectors of American higher education, such as liberal arts colleges, comprehensive universities, and community colleges. Institutions such as the University of New Hampshire developed teaching certificates for those intending to work in colleges and universities. A number of individual universities and foundations have picked up on this important agenda.

A Pedagogical Revolution

By the second half of the 1990s it was clear that a fundamental pedagogical change was taking place in U.S. higher education and that the teaching role was being transformed. Collaborative learning, experience-based learning, and technologically assisted instruction were challenging the pedagogical assumptions that have been taken for granted for so long. It is now widely acknowledged that faculty no longer have full responsibility for the transfer of knowledge. This pedagogical revolution was being effectively urged on by research on how people learn. The prestigious National Research Council launched a publication effort that documented and disseminated broadly what was being discovered about learning from the cognitive sciences, psychology, education, and other disciplines. A new interdisciplinary field called the science of learning is being established.

What is being learned about the power of collaborative learning is being institutionalized by the national learning communities movement, coordinated through the Washington Center for Improving the Quality of Undergraduate Education (Olympia, Washington). Classes are being recruited and organized with the intent of forming cohort teams, and we now acknowledge and intentionally build on what students learn from peers. As we draw on what we now know about the effectiveness of active learning, in-depth learning is regularly expected to take place in co-op settings and on student internships. What is called service learning has become a movement centered at the Campus Compact, a president-initiated organization, reaching across the disciplines. Technologically assisted learning has proven to be particularly effective in the sciences, engineering, and mathematics. The National Academy of Sciences and the Howard Hughes Medical Institute grant a large number of lucrative teaching awards to individual faculty that virtually all build on technological innovation.

The search for best practices in university teaching has been an elusive one. The most popular resource on the subject to date is Chickering and Gamson's "Seven Principles for Good Practice in Undergraduate Education." They conclude that good teaching:

1. Encourages contact between students and faculty
2. Develops reciprocity and cooperation among students
3. Uses active learning techniques
4. Gives prompt feedback
5. Emphasizes time on task
6. Communicates high expectations
7. Respects diverse talents and ways of learning

The Johnson Foundation (a corporate foundation) supported development and broad dissemination of these principles. Most of the teaching initiatives launched recently in U.S. colleges and universities have built on what is encapsulated here (Chickering and Gamson, 1987).

A Broader Definition of Scholarship

Over the past twenty years, no effort to enhance the quality of teaching in U.S. higher education has received more attention than the attempt to broaden the dominant understanding of the scholarly work of faculty—what counts as scholarship. In 1990, the Carnegie Foundation for the Advancement of Teaching published *Scholarship Reconsidered: Priorities of the Professoriate* (Boyer, 1990). The book had great influence and remains the foundation's most widely disseminated publication. Fifteen years later, another study tracing the impact of that effort and the subsequent initiatives it ignited has appeared, titled *Faculty Priorities Reconsidered: Rewarding Multiple Forms of Scholarship* (O'Meara and Rice, 2005). The primary focus of this whole endeavor was to realign the priorities of the American professoriate with the essential missions of the nation's colleges and universities—to redefine faculty roles and restructure reward systems. Nationally, most of the work concentrated on making teaching a scholarly enterprise, one that is recognized and honored as such. In addition to the scholarship of

NEW DIRECTIONS FOR HIGHER EDUCATION • DOI 10.1002/he

discovery, its integration, and application, the major emphasis is on the scholarship of teaching and learning. To encourage this endeavor and offer national coordination, the American Association for Higher Education launched the Forum on Faculty Roles and Rewards. The Carnegie Foundation, under the intellectual leadership of Lee Schulman, extended the work with campuses and academic disciplines through the Carnegie Academy for the Scholarship of Teaching and Learning (CASTL). Most recently, an active International Association for the Scholarship of Teaching and Learning has been formed to advance this agenda.

The federal agency that is presently working most effectively to enhance the quality of teaching in American colleges and universities is the National Science Foundation (NSF). Recently, NSF generously funded a Center for the Integration of Research, Teaching, and Learning (CIRTL), located at the University of Wisconsin, Madison, and working in collaboration with Pennsylvania State University (Penn State) and Michigan State University. The center concentrates on working with graduate students preparing to teach in the sciences, engineering, and mathematics across the several sectors of higher education. In the United States, the scholarly priorities of the professoriate are firmly rooted in graduate school socialization. Enhancing the quality of teaching in the university must begin there.

A Critical Challenge

Over the years, American higher education has thrived on a vision of the teacher-scholar, the complete scholar. This ideal conception of the faculty role fosters institutional coherence and a sense of the whole in a time of dramatic change. This vision is now being challenged, both from within U.S. institutions and from abroad. In the United States, new for-profit universities such as the highly successful University of Phoenix have joined others in intentionally seeking to unbundle the faculty role. Instructional technology is a primary driver behind much of this development. Teams of academic experts—not all of whom are faculty—design online courses in a digital environment in a way that makes role differentiation not only possible but perhaps inevitable. Many other countries do not even use the term *faculty* to refer to the individual teacher. The United Kingdom's Open University, for instance, has been engaged in this kind of team-based course design for years and has demonstrated its effectiveness. The content specialist is just one among several academic staff who contribute to the instructional process.

In the American context, we have taken an additive approach to the improvement of teaching. New reforms have added to the responsibilities of teaching faculty. In interviews with early-career faculty across the country, new teachers regularly complain about what is being added to an already (in their words) "overloaded plate." There is widespread concern that we are developing an academic career that is no longer viable and will not attract the best talent into the teaching profession. Reorganizing the teaching function itself is called for.

In the past several decades much has been done to enhance the quality of teaching in U.S. colleges and universities. Significant gains have been made in focusing attention on the importance of student learning. The emerging challenge is to rethink how the teaching role has been structured and instruction is delivered. U.S. higher education has much to learn from a comparative approach.

References

Altbach, P. G., Berdahl, R. O., and Gumport, P. J. (eds.), *American Higher Education in the Twenty-First Century: Social, Political, and Economic Challenges.* Baltimore: Johns Hopkins University Press, 1999.

Boyer, E. *Scholarship Reconsidered: Priorities of the Professoriate.* Princeton, N.J.: Carnegie Foundation for the Advancement of Teaching, 1990.

Chickering, A. W., and Gamson, Z. F. "Seven Principles of Good Practice in Undergraduate Education." *AAHE Bulletin,* 1987, *39*(7), 3–7.

Gerth, H. H., and Mills, C. W. (eds.). *Max Weber: Essays in Sociology.* Oxford: Oxford University Press, 1946.

Jenks, C., and Riesman, D. *The Academic Revolution.* Garden City, N.Y.: Doubleday, 1968.

O'Meara, K. A., and Rice, R. E. (eds.). *Faculty Priorities Reconsidered: Rewarding Multiple Forms of Scholarship.* San Francisco: Jossey-Bass, 2005.

Rice, R. E. "The Future of the American Faculty: An Interview with Martin J. Finkelstein and Jack H. Schuster." *Change,* 2005, *36*(2), 26–35.

Sweezy v. *New Hampshire,* 354 U.S. 234 (1957).

R. EUGENE RICE is a senior scholar at the Association of American Colleges and Universities in Washington, D.C.

3

Multiple jurisdictions engender variegated governance procedures for improving quality in the universities of Canada.

Enhancing the Quality of Teaching in Canada

Janet Gail Donald

Canada has a significant investment in postsecondary education: more than half the population of some thirty-two million people have a postsecondary certificate, degree, or degrees (Statistics Canada, 2004, cited in Canadian Association of University Teachers, 2005). The size of the country, extending over six time zones, sets the context for social development in the ten provinces and the territories. There is no federal ministry of education or formal accreditation system; the provinces have jurisdiction over their universities. The Canadian constitution, enacted in 1867 as the British North America Act and revised in 1982, awards authority to the federal government for defense and trade but authority to the provinces for health, education, and language. Although funding for postsecondary education is primarily in the form of transfer payments from the federal to the provincial governments, which have vested responsibility for all levels of education, the provincial governments allocate funds to the universities. The federal government reserves the right to fund research and support students. In response to the diversity of needs in the regions, responsibility and accountability are distributed among the provinces and individual institutions. Thus the pilot question in this volume of how trends of economic globalization and increased performance accountability in higher education have affected the enhancement of teaching and learning in Canada over the past thirty years must be read through the lens of decentralized authority and hence responsibility.

NEW DIRECTIONS FOR HIGHER EDUCATION, no. 133, Spring 2006 © Wiley Periodicals, Inc.
Published online in Wiley InterScience (www.interscience.wiley.com) • DOI: 10.1002/he.202

The Range of Postsecondary Educational Institutions

The provinces and territories vary widely in size and population and in the kind of postsecondary education offered. According to the Association of Universities and Colleges of Canada (AUCC), which represents the universities, as of July 2005 there were ninety-one member universities and university colleges (AUCC, 2005). The most populated provinces— Ontario, with more than one-third of the population (twelve million), and Quebec, with one-quarter (seven and a half million)—have twenty-nine and nineteen universities, respectively; other provinces have from one (Prince Edward Island and Newfoundland) to eleven (in British Columbia). In five provinces there are English language and French language institutions, with some universities offering instruction in both official languages. In addition, there are more than two hundred community colleges, two of which provide higher education in the Yukon and Northwest Territories. The universities offer more than ten thousand undergraduate and graduate degree programs as well as professional degree programs and certificates.

Research is carried out at all Canadian universities despite the range of size and mission. Although the AUCC treats all universities as equal, universities are differentiated into three categories in a de facto annual evaluation carried out by Canada's weekly news magazine, *Maclean's* (Johnston and Dwyer, 2003). Among the forty-seven universities participating in this assessment, in the "medical doctoral" category fifteen universities offer a broad range of doctoral programs and research including medicine; the largest has forty-eight thousand full-time students. The eleven "comprehensive" universities are defined as having a significant amount of research activity and a wide range of programs at undergraduate and graduate levels, including professional degrees. The twenty-one "primarily undergraduate" universities have relatively few graduate programs, with as many as twelve thousand or as few as two thousand students. Of the fifteen medical doctoral universities, six are located in Ontario, four in Quebec, one in each of the four western provinces, and one in Nova Scotia. These institutions would be considered "research intensive," although only the two earliest established universities, the University of Toronto and McGill University, are members of the Association of American Universities.

Funding also varies widely. In 2003, eighteen universities had an endowment of over $100 million Canadian, the largest with more than $1 billion, allowing some degree of financial flexibility (Canadian Association of University Business Officers, 2004, cited in Canadian Association of University Teachers, 2005). However, on average 60 percent of university operating revenue was from government funds, 30 percent from tuition. Tuition varies with provincial policy, but the average tuition for arts programs in 2004 was less than $4,000, while for medicine it was over $9,000 and for dentistry tuition over $11,000 (Statistics Canada, n.d., cited in

Canadian Association of University Teachers, 2005). The range in tuition for arts students, for example, was from under $2,000 in Quebec to over $5,700 in Nova Scotia. Approximately 40 percent of full-time university students received a student loan from the federal government in 2000 (Statistics Canada, Sept. 2004a), and Human Resources Development Canada, Review of the Government of Canada's Student Financial Assistance Program (Human Resources Development Canada, 2002, cited in Canadian Association of University Teachers, 2005). In terms of governance, universities are generally considered autonomous institutions, for the most part with a corporate board of governors that has responsibility for administrative and financial matters and a senate responsible for academic matters (Jones, 1997). Given such a widespread and diverse array of institutions, development of accreditation processes has been a matter of long-term negotiation.

Performance Accountability Across Canada

One foundational index of accountability is accreditation, that is, official recognition that an institution is meeting minimum standards of curriculum, staff qualifications, and resources (Adelman, 1992). In Canada this is accomplished through membership in the AUCC combined with each university's provincial government charter. The Website for AUCC states that universities design their own mission and pursue their own future but cooperate with one another and work collectively. To be an accredited member, each institution must meet a set of criteria (AUCC, 2002):

• Have an approved, clearly articulated, and widely known and accepted mission statement and academic goals that are appropriate to a university and that demonstrate its commitment to: (1) teaching and other forms of dissemination of knowledge; (2) research, scholarship, academic inquiry, and the advancement of knowledge; and (3) service to the community.
• Have as its core teaching mission provision of education of university standard with the majority of its programs at that level.
• Offer a full program or programs of undergraduate and/or graduate studies that animate its mission and goals, and that lead to a university degree or degrees.
• Undergraduate degree programs are characterized by breadth and depth in the traditional areas of the liberal arts and sciences; first degrees of a professional nature, such as medicine, law, teacher education, and engineering, have a significant liberal arts or science component.
• Have a proven record of scholarship, academic inquiry, and research; it expects academic staff to be engaged in externally peer reviewed research and to publish in externally disseminated sources; and it provides appropriate time and institutional support for them to do so. Indicators of this commitment will include policies and programs pertaining to

creation of knowledge, development of curriculum, and execution of research projects.

• Have a governance and administrative structure appropriate to a university, including authority vested in academic staff for decisions affecting academic programs including admissions, content, graduation requirements and standards, and related policies and procedures through membership on an elected senate or other appropriate elected body representative of academic staff.

The criteria are applied to any university seeking membership in the AUCC and therefore serve as a basic standard for Canadian universities. Degree accreditation is, however, a provincial responsibility, and the provinces and territories have resisted federal government attempts to be more involved in educational decisions (Cameron, 1997; Marshall, 2004). Each province has developed its own procedures for approval of new institutions and credentials, and for quality assurance. To begin on the east coast: Newfoundland has one university established by the province's Memorial University Act; it has an internal process of self-study and review with program reviews every seven years (Marshall, 2004). In the three maritime provinces, the University of Prince Edward Island and the four universities in New Brunswick have an internal program review, but all new program proposals and significant changes to programs are reviewed by the Maritime Provinces Higher Education Commission (MPHEC). In neighboring Nova Scotia, the ten universities have internal program review processes, the Nova Scotia Advisory Board reviews new regional programs, and the MPHEC reviews all new program proposals. Thus the maritime provinces coordinate new program review.

In Quebec, although AUCC accredits nineteen universities, eleven of them form the University of Quebec, a system of regional universities. Individual institutions set periodic program assessment policy that is reviewed by the Conference of Rectors and Principals of Quebec Universities (CREPUQ). For example, McGill University instituted a cyclical program review process in the early 1980s; in 1992, graduates from the previous ten years were invited to evaluate their program, teaching and student life, and the relevance of their studies to experiences after graduation, for use in quality assurance and program improvement (Donald and Denison, 1996). In Ontario, quality assurance for the twenty-nine universities follows a differentiated pattern: academic peer review, internal cyclical reviews of departments and programs, a provincial Undergraduate Program Review Committee, and the Ontario Council on Graduate Studies for graduate program appraisal. The Ontario government introduced key performance indicators during the 1990s to determine a component of each university's operating grant (Jones, 2004).

In the four universities in Manitoba, all new program proposals are reviewed by another institution in the province that offers the same program; approval is from the Council on Postsecondary Education, and quality is also monitored by graduate satisfaction surveys and student in-class surveys. Saskatchewan, although it has six AUCC accredited universities, does not have an external program review process other than for professional accreditation. The University of Saskatchewan does, however, have an exemplary program review process (Banta and Donald, 2004). In Alberta, the six AUCC-accredited universities have internal program review procedures, and new programs are assessed by a Quality Assurance Council. British Columbia's eleven universities and university colleges have internal review procedures and submit new program proposals to the BC ministry for approval.

Thus a variety of intermediary bodies, some university councils as in Quebec and some under provincial jurisdiction, determine whether new programs and revisions are permitted. Across the country, quality assurance occurs at three levels: the individual institution's program review process, some form of provincial or interprovincial accreditation process, and membership in AUCC. Some Canadian scholars have suggested that university reform in Canada and elsewhere could be seen as the imposition of a new "market ideology" on universities that has had the effect of deregulating postsecondary education but at the same time demanding greater quality control and accountability (Schuetze and Bruneau, 2004). I would argue that given Canada's variegated regional contexts, rather than "regulation," accountability is operationalized as a mixture of self-governance and cooperation. The accountability structures and processes described here do not communicate whether economic globalization has been a cause, nor how the quality or enhancement of university teaching and learning has been affected in Canada. Although some of the same actors are involved in the process of enhancing teaching, what follows is a substantially different narrative.

Teaching Quality

The earliest recorded attempt in Canada to understand academic quality was a cross-Canada study of university teachers' views on teaching expertise. Winners of university teaching awards were asked to describe how they taught; many reported that it was an extremely difficult assignment to describe their instructional process (Sheffield, 1974). Most found it hard to define *teaching,* let alone creativity in teaching. Their strongest point of agreement was that the teacher's most important role was to stimulate students to become active learners on their own. They also agreed on the importance of subject mastery, preparation, and interacting with students. The study did not, however, broach the question of how to ensure teaching quality.

New Directions for Higher Education • DOI 10.1002/he

The question of quality and accountability in universities became more acute over the next two decades. In 1990 the AUCC established an independent Commission of Inquiry on Canadian University Education to review the educational function of Canada's universities and to find ways by which universities could ensure that their educational programs were of high quality (Donald, 1991). In one study done for the commission, on the quality of teaching, representatives of each university were asked to rate the importance of nineteen criteria for assessing faculty performance (Donald and Saroyan, 1991). The representatives assigned high importance to six criteria: research productivity, teaching competence, being up to date in the subject matter, having an academic degree, effective communication skills, and the ability to obtain research funds. Thus both research and teaching quality were critical indicators of faculty performance.

Large and small universities differed, however, in the relative attention paid to research and teaching. Ninety-one percent of the large universities considered research productivity of high importance, while 61 percent of the small universities did so. The percentage was almost reversed for teaching competence; 62 percent of the large universities considered it of high importance compared with 96 percent of the small universities. Few universities large or small attached high importance to innovative activities such as participating in continuing professional development, being a change agent, multidisciplinarity, or computer and technology literacy. In summary, large or more research-intensive universities allocated greater importance to research than to teaching. The commission concluded that although university policies supported excellence in teaching, research, and service, there were large variations by institution and by discipline in the importance given to each area and in the combination of duties that professors undertake. The commission perceived a deep cynicism among faculty concerning the real importance accorded teaching.

More than a decade later, the performance measures for faculty in the *Maclean's* ranking of universities focus on research rather than on teaching (Johnston and Dwyer, 2003). The measures include the number of faculty with a Ph.D. (weighted 3 percent), the number of national awards (3 percent), and the number and size of research grants (11 percent of the overall weight). The performance measures closest to teaching are class size and classes taught by tenured faculty (17 to 18 percent weighting). No direct measures are made of teaching quality despite an extensive literature available on the process.

Initiatives to Enhance University Teaching and Learning

In the study on the quality of teaching done for the AUCC Commission, a variety of resources and facilities were found at universities for improving teaching, although the frequency of any one kind of resource was not high

(Donald and Saroyan, 1991). The most common resource was a university committee on teaching (44 percent), followed by a center for the improvement of teaching (41 percent) and peer consultants (22 percent). Large universities reported having more resources for improving teaching: more centers for the improvement of teaching (64 percent versus 19 percent), more university committees on teaching (57 percent versus 31 percent), and greater access to counselors for the improvement of teaching (36 percent versus 12 percent). The commission concluded that teaching assistants and doctoral candidates should be given some training in teaching and supervised opportunities to practice their teaching skills. The commission also concluded that student ratings should be universal, conducted seriously, and taken seriously, but that they should not constitute the only method of evaluating teaching. The inquiry served as a benchmark for teaching and learning practice in Canadian universities; still, one unexpected consequence was that it appeared to effect closure and end discussion on what should be done to improve postsecondary instruction.

What initiatives have been taken since that time? In 2005, the Website for the Canadian Society for the Study of Higher Education (CSSHE) listed seven higher education programs in Canada and twenty university teaching and learning centers or services across the country. The Society for Teaching and Learning in Higher Education (STLHE), formed in the 1980s to give professors a venue to talk about their teaching, aspires to be a strong advocate for enhancement of teaching and learning in Canada. Each society holds an annual meeting to discuss issues of quality in Canadian higher education. It is also evident that attention to enhancing teaching, instead of increasing from the previous two decades, has undergone a change in direction. In some universities, administrative steps have been taken to aid professors in documenting their teaching development in teaching portfolios for purposes of promotion and tenure; other universities have introduced alternative career paths that allow professors to concentrate on their teaching. Workshops are still offered at universities both large and small for the improvement of teaching. At the same time, universities appear to be investing less in the substantive research needed to explore teaching and learning in postsecondary education. At the level of administrative policy, criteria for teaching effectiveness are clearer. There is also organization to support the "scholarship" of teaching, that is, provision for professors to talk about their teaching. Whether scholarship will lead to or include rigorous, substantive research remains to be determined.

The Context in the Twenty-First Century

Canadian universities' combined hiring needs are projected to be between twenty-five hundred and three thousand new faculty per year over the next ten years, compared with fewer than one thousand faculty per year in recent years (Elliot, 2000). This projection is based on an expected increase in student enrollment of 20 percent owing to demographic and participation rate increase, and the need to replace retiring faculty in greater numbers. In Organization for Economic and Co-operation and Development (OECD) projections, the average age of Canadian university professors was forty-nine, generally older than the average in other OECD countries; only half of departing faculty in Canada have been replaced in the last several years. From 1991 to 2001, the number of full-time professors fell from 32,700 to 30,800; the student-faculty ratio rose from 17.5 to 22.9 (Statistics Canada, Centre for Education Statistics, various reports cited in Canadian Association of University Teachers, 2005). Budget cuts during the last decade have translated into heavier teaching loads, larger class sizes, and reduced administrative support. At the same time, there are increased demands for foundation or first-year programs, undergraduate programs that involve students in research, and interdisciplinary programs. This places increasing expectations on today's professors, and competition among universities. The board of the AUCC recently released a statement applauding the federal government program for authorizing funding to repatriate top Canadian researchers and to keep the best researchers in Canada, but it also stated the need to continue to build on a vision that allows leveraging of people, partnerships, and resources in a global talent race for the best researchers (AUCC, 2005). The focus of administrators in Canadian universities is indeed on continuing to compete with other countries, making investments in research, people, and infrastructure in the global knowledge society.

Over the past thirty years in Canada, the trend was first to examine excellence in teaching, and then the quality of postsecondary education, to come to the recognition that Canada's universities are underresourced to meet the demands of an inquiry-oriented society. To meet this challenge, substantive research is needed on how to help postsecondary students learn: examining how students encode knowledge in different disciplines, furnishing students with models in the disciplines they are studying, and studying what instructional methods and approaches best support higher-order learning. Identifying critical issues that need to be addressed in Canada to enhance university teaching and learning is complicated by the multitude of jurisdictions and a benign but laissez-faire philosophy of autonomy and cooperation. The chief issue would appear to be the importance accorded learning and its enhancement by university administrators. The increased emphasis and accompanying funding given to research across Canada is laudable, but more research is needed on postsecondary teaching and learning.

References

Adelman, C. "Accreditation." In B. R. Clark and G. R. Neave (eds.), *The Encyclopedia of Higher Education*. Oxford: Pergamon Press, 1992.

Association of Universities and Colleges of Canada. "About AUCC Membership Eligibility." 2002. http://www.aucc.ca/publications/media.
Association of Universities and Colleges of Canada (AUCC). 2005. http://www.aucc.ca/.
Banta, T., and Donald, J. G. *University of Saskatchewan Systematic Program Review Report.* Saskatoon: University of Saskatchewan, 2004.
Cameron, D. M. "The Federal Perspective." In G. Jones (ed.), *Higher Education in Canada: Different Systems, Different Perspectives.* New York: Garland, 1997.
Canadian Association of University Business Officers. University Investment Survey. May 2004. http://www.acpau.ca/index_e.cfm.
Canadian Association of University Teachers. "CAUT Almanac of Post-Secondary Education in Canada." 2005. http://www.caut.ca.
Canadian Society for the Study of Higher Education. http://umanitoba.ca/outreach/csshe.
Donald, J. G. "The Commission of Inquiry on Canadian University Education: The Quality and Evaluation of Teaching." *Interamericana de Gestion y Lederazgo Universitario,* 1991, *1,* 157–173.
Donald, J. G., and Denison, D. B. "Evaluating Undergraduate Education: The Use of Broad Indicators." *Assessment and Evaluation in Higher Education,* 1996, *21*(1), 23–39.
Donald, J. G., and Saroyan, A. *Assessing the Quality of Teaching in Canadian Universities.* Research report no. 3. Ottawa: AUCC Commission of Inquiry on Canadian University Education, 1991.
Elliot, L. *Revitalizing Universities Through Faculty Renewal.* Research File 4(1). Association of Universities and Colleges of Canada, Mar. 2000.
Human Resources Development Canada. Review of the Government of Canada's Student Financial Assistance Programs: Canada Student Loans Program 2001–2002. Ottawa, Ontario: Human Resources Development Canada, 2002.
Johnston, A. D., and Dwyer, M. "Ranking Canadian Universities." *Maclean's,* Nov. 17, 2003, pp. 40–41.
Jones, G. (ed.). *Higher Education in Canada: Different Systems, Different Perspectives.* New York: Garland, 1997.
Jones, G. "Ontario Higher Education Reform, 1995–2003: From Modest Modifications to Policy Reform." *Canadian Journal of Higher Education,* 2004, *34*(3), 39–54.
Marshall, D. "Degree Accreditation in Canada." *Canadian Journal of Higher Education,* 2004, *34*(2), 69–96.
Schuetze, H., and Bruneau, W. "Less State, More Market: University Reform in Canada and Abroad." *Canadian Journal of Higher Education,* 2004, *34*(3), 1–12.
Sheffield, E. F. *Teaching in the Universities: No One Way.* Montreal: McGill-Queen's University Press, 1974.
Society for Teaching and Learning in Higher Education. http://www.tss.uoguelph.ca/STLHE.
Statistics Canada. Access, Persistence and Financing: First Results from the Postsecondary Participation Survey, Sept. 2004. http://www.statcan.ca/start.html.
Statistics Canada. Labour Force Survey, special tabulation, Oct. 2004. http://www.statcan.ca/start.html.
Statistics Canada, Centre for Education Statistics. Tuition and Living Accommodation Costs Survey, n.d. http://www.statcan.ca/start.html.

JANET GAIL DONALD is professor emeritus at McGill University and a Fellow of the Royal Society of Canada.

In Australia a major national reform of universities is currently under way that is resulting in tension between government control and market forces.

Enhancing the Quality of Teaching: An Australian Perspective

John M. Dearn

Like most countries, Australia is currently experiencing a period of great change in its higher education sector. These changes are being driven by both the growing importance of higher education as a major factor determining national economic prosperity and a growing demand on the part of individuals for flexible and lifelong access to higher education. Underlying these changes are innovations in information and communication technologies that have transformed how we can access and share information.

The changes being experienced by higher education in Australia can be considered in terms of three central issues. The first is the tension between private benefit versus public good, an issue of particular significance in Australia, where the higher education system is almost entirely public. Although individuals clearly benefit from higher education, governments (national and state) also want to have a major say about what is taught in our universities in addressing social and economic priorities. This tension underlies argument about who should pay for higher education, who should determine program provision and curricula, and who should determine standards. A key feature of Australian higher education is the anomaly that universities are almost all public but are self-accrediting institutions and enjoy a high degree of autonomy with respect to many aspects of their activities, including curricula, entry standards, and the range of programs they provide.

The second current issue in Australian higher education is the relationship among universities, higher education, and vocational education

NEW DIRECTIONS FOR HIGHER EDUCATION, no. 133, Spring 2006 © Wiley Periodicals, Inc.
Published online in Wiley InterScience (www.interscience.wiley.com) • DOI: 10.1002/he.203

and training. Even though higher education is furnished predominantly by universities, there is increasing delivery by private providers; they potentially threaten the long-held monopoly enjoyed by public universities. Private providers operate under quite different educational models and could better meet the needs of adult learners who are combining study with work and family commitments. In addition, postsecondary education in Australia also has a vocational education and training (VET) sector, which operates in parallel with higher education. VET is delivered in the workplace and also in technical and further education (TAFE) colleges. In recent years, there has been increasing demand for pathways between the sectors, in particular from TAFE colleges to universities; and in a new development, requests are coming from within the VET sector to be able to offer a bachelor's degree in direct competition with universities. A complicating factor is that universities are managed by the Commonwealth government, but VET and TAFE colleges are funded and managed by the state and territorial governments.

The third issue is the relationship among the teaching, scholarship, and research activities of universities. Recent Australian Commonwealth government reforms have made a clear distinction among these activities regarding how universities are funded and managed. A forthcoming national research assessment exercise has the potential to further force a distinction between teaching and research in our universities. The role of research in higher education teaching has been, of course, a longstanding and contentious issue in higher education, and the outcome of the current debate in Australia may significantly affect the quality of higher education and the nature of academic work.

Underlying all three of these issues in Australia has been the theme of the quality of learning and teaching, both quality improvement and quality assurance—though, as will be explored, exactly what is meant by quality in higher education learning and teaching is far from uncontested.

The Higher Education System in Australia

Australia currently has forty institutions recognized as universities, of which thirty-seven are considered public and three private (AVCC, 2005). However, given that for the public universities only some 44 percent of operating revenue currently comes from government sources (down from 90 percent in 1981), just what is meant by "public" in the context of Australian higher education is an interesting notion. The current set of universities emerged following creation of the Unified National System at the end of the 1980s, which ended the previous binary system in which higher education was delivered through universities and colleges of advanced education (DEET, 1993).

Compared with other countries, Australian universities are relatively homogeneous with all of them offering doctoral programs and claiming to be research-intensive. However, research performance, at least as measured by conventional criteria, is highly variable, and a forthcoming national research audit may well result in formal recognition of a number of university types on the basis of their mix of teaching, basic research, and applied research. Indeed, over recent years four groups of universities have emerged, the most recent being the "new generation universities," consisting of a group of new institutions with a particular focus on community engagement, cross-disciplinary programs, and applied research.

The size of Australian universities in terms of full-time-equivalent students varies with about equal numbers of institutions below ten thousand, between ten thousand and twenty thousand, and over twenty thousand (AVCC, 2005). There are currently 929,952 students (650,850 full-time equivalent) studying in Australian universities (AVCC, 2005, 2003 figures). The huge growth in university participation in Australia in recent years can be seen in the fact that in 1994 this figure was only 585,435 (Nelson, 2004). Among individuals age fifteen to sixty-four, the current overall participation rate in higher education is 13 percent. As of 2003, 18 percent of Australians age fifteen to sixty-four have a bachelor's degree or higher, up from only 10 percent in 1992.

Of the current student population, 27.3 percent are over thirty, 21.4 percent are part-time, and 15.1 percent are studying in external (distance) mode. Fifty-five percent are domestic undergraduate students, and 19 percent domestic postgraduate. Overseas undergraduates make up 13 percent, while overseas postgraduate students represent 8 percent. There were (in 2004) 33,043 full-time equivalent academic staff in Australian universities, giving an overall ratio of students to academic staff of 20.8, up from 14.2 in 1993 (AVCC, 2005).

Funding of Australian Higher Education

Public expenditure on higher education in 2001 in Australia amounted to 0.8 percent of GDP, which is comparable with the United Kingdom (also at 0.8 percent) but lower than, for instance, Finland (at 1.7 percent) and Denmark (1.8 percent; AVCC, 2005). However, interesting differences between Australia and other countries emerge when the proportion of funding on tertiary education that comes from public sources is examined. Australia's public contribution is 51.3 percent, lower than the United Kingdom (71.0 percent) and considerably lower than Denmark (97.8 percent), Finland (96.5 percent), and Greece (99.6 percent; AVCC, 2005).

In absolute terms, the expenditure on higher education by the Australian Commonwealth government in 2005 was about Aus. $5 billion. Of this amount, about $3 billion is from the Commonwealth Grant Scheme (CGS), which funds undergraduate teaching. The amount each institution receives under the CGS is determined by its agreed number of domestic undergraduate places across the disciplinary fields. The remaining $2 billion of the CGS is used to fund such items as research, research training, research infrastructure equity programs, quality improvement initiatives, and scholarships. However, the research, research training, and research infrastructure funds are all performance-based; their distribution across institutions is quite skewed, with the older research intensive universities capturing a high proportion of the funds.

Higher Education in Australia: Central Control Versus Market Forces?

Perhaps the central issue for higher education in Australia currently is the tension between central management by the Commonwealth government and decision making by individual institutions on the basis of market forces—the market in this case being primarily student demand for higher education courses and to a lesser degree employers and the professions. Nevertheless, the nature of this "market" in Australia is complex and not easily characterized in terms of public versus private.

The Commonwealth government allocates a number of domestic undergraduate student places to each university. In a new development, these places are being allocated to specific discipline areas (for example, humanities or engineering). The number of places in each discipline area represents a target that has to be met by individual institutions through their admission process, with financial penalties applying to universities that end up with too few or too many students in each discipline area. Thus the distribution of students across institutions may not necessarily reflect real student preference, with institutions protected from direct competition.

The profile of student places allocated across disciplines for each institution is subject to annual negotiation between each university and the Commonwealth government. These negotiations take into account the strategic direction of the individual institution as well as local demographic and employment trends. A particular point of interest is the perspectives brought to the negotiation by the Commonwealth government in contrast to an institution, which might wish to change its profile (notably closure of particular programs) according to such internal factors as student demand, costs, and staffing availability. By contrast, the Commonwealth government criteria would include national economic and social needs. The resulting tension is currently being addressed by the government, which has suggested that universities should notify the government of any intention to close a program, although how the government would address continuance of an unprofitable though important program at an individual institution is unclear.

The tension between the private and public roles of higher education is also seen in who pays for undergraduate higher education. The current Australian model for funding undergraduate education sees benefit flowing to both individuals and society. This is reflected in the relative payments made by the government on the one hand and individuals on the other. The current model is strongly prescriptive. For example, for a place in an undergraduate law course a university receives a payment from the Commonwealth government of Aus. $1,472 per year. In addition, however, the student is required to pay Aus. $8,018 per year. On the other hand, the university receives $8,869 per annum for a student place in a foreign language course, while the student contribution is only $4,808 per annum.

Two points are worth noting. First, the student contribution can be paid back through an income-contingent loan scheme through the Commonwealth taxation system with no up-front payment required. Second, and different from the situation in many other countries, the costs and payments are uniform across all institutions—a reflection of the English tradition of higher education in which universities are deemed to be of equivalent standard.

In a recent development, in an attempt to open up the market to more competition, universities can admit undergraduate students in addition to the agreed number of Commonwealth-supported places on a full-fee-paying basis. This is clearly a potential risk with respect to quality and involves a level of trust that universities will not lower admission standards in return for additional income. However, in another policy twist that challenges the notion of anything like a free market for higher education in Australia, the number of full-fee-paying students must not exceed 35 percent of the total enrollment in the course. Furthermore, in an attempt to introduce competition, institutions are able to charge an additional 25 percent on top of the agreed base-level student contribution for the discipline. Not surprisingly, almost every university has done just that.

One might expect demand for higher education in Australia to have been affected by recent sharp increases in costs, but this does not appear to be the case (Nelson, 2005). Perhaps the income-contingent loan scheme has generated a credit card mentality, where the impact of financial commitments is not fully appreciated at the time. Alternatively, it might be that access to higher education is valued regardless of cost. Though not apparently diminishing demand for higher education, it is clear that introducing substantial student fees has created a more consumer-focused student population with increased expectations relative to service and value for money. One impact of this development has been introduction of diverse teaching and learning strategies under the umbrella term "flexible learning," usually involving educational technologies and in particular Web-based access to learning resources.

In contrast to undergraduate education, postgraduate coursework programs in Australia receive insignificant Commonwealth support; students—most of whom are in the workforce—are required to pay the full cost of their course themselves, though in many cases this cost is met at least in part by their employer. Introduction of flexible delivery modes of educational delivery such as online courses and block teaching has been most marked in the case of postgraduate programs designed to meet the needs of learners who are combining study with work and family responsibilities.

Focus on the Quality of Learning and Teaching

At the same time as major changes have been implemented in how higher education is financed, there is an intense national focus on the issue of quality in higher education. This is not a new development; a major review of quality in higher education was conducted in 1992 (HEC, 1992), leading to a series of quality reviews. Nevertheless, a renewed focus on quality in the late 1990s led to establishment of the Australian Quality Assurance Framework (DETYA, 2000). This initiative can be seen as a response to both the lack of any form of external accreditation of universities and the specter of new institutions establishing themselves in Australia and appropriating the name "university."

The Australian Higher Education Quality Assurance Framework consists of four elements. First, there are a set of protocols that all universities are required to meet in order to ensure consistent criteria and standards across Australia with respect to such issues as the criteria and processes for recognition of universities. These include, for example, a requirement that universities demonstrate (1) teaching and learning that engages with advanced knowledge and inquiry; (2) a culture of sustained scholarship extending from what informs inquiry and basic teaching and learning to creation of new knowledge through research and original creative endeavor; and (3) commitment of teachers, researchers, course designers, and assessors to free inquiry and systematic advancement of knowledge.

The second element is the Australian Qualifications Framework (AQF), which describes the nature and standards of fourteen national educational awards, among them the bachelor's degree, master's degree, and doctoral degree. The third element is the annual negotiations between the Commonwealth government and individual universities with respect to (1) allocation of Commonwealth-supported student places and (2) their sustainability, achievements, quality outcomes, and compliance in what is known as the Institution Assessment Framework bilateral discussions.

The final element of the Australian Higher Education Quality Assurance Framework was establishment of the Australian Universities Quality Agency (AUQA), which conducts five yearly whole-institution public audits of universities on the basis of a portfolio prepared by the university, complemented by a site visit. The focus of AUQA is on identifying evidence of quality improvement through the existence of good planning, implementation, and review processes.

Current Developments

Notwithstanding establishment of the Australian Higher Education Quality Assurance Framework in 2000, the Commonwealth government—which controls higher education in Australia—initiated a major review of higher education in 2002, which has led to a series of significant reforms affecting all areas of university activity.

At the commencement of the review, the Commonwealth government made clear the need for a higher education system that was, to use its own words, value-adding, learner-centered, high-quality, equitable, responsive, diverse, innovative, flexible, cost-effective, publicly accountable, and socially responsible (Nelson, 2002). Though not stating it as such, the current Commonwealth government clearly was of the opinion that Australian universities were not cost-effective, sufficiently accountable, learner-centered or responsive, and so on.

The consultation process that was conducted as part of the review identified a number of concerns, including the high cost of course provision, duplication of courses across institutions that individually have low enrollment, continued underrepresentation of students from disadvantaged backgrounds, and a high proportion of students who do not complete their university program.

The current reform package is addressing a number of issues related to financing, staffing, and governance of universities, in particular changes to how students access and pay for higher education. Perhaps the change that will prove to have the greatest long-term significance in Australia is explicit separation, in the Commonwealth funding given to universities, between that for research and that for what is termed teaching and scholarship. The earlier assumption that all teaching staff in Australian universities are also engaged in research, which was implicit in the previous funding model, no longer holds, though what is meant by scholarship is yet to be determined.

In the area of learning and teaching, four major initiatives are being implemented, aimed at raising both the status of university teaching and the quality of student learning.

The first is establishment of a national institute for learning and teaching, which will be a national focus for enhancement of learning and teaching in Australia. Called the Carrick Institute for Learning and Teaching in Higher Education, it begins operation in 2006.

The institute will operate through various programs of national teaching fellowships, funded projects and learning, teaching grants, and so on. The work of the Carrick Institute will build on that of its predecessors, the Committee for the Advancement of University Teaching (CAUT), the Committee for University Teaching and Staff Development (CUTSD), and the Australian

Universities Teaching Committee (AUTC). The institute will also manage the second major learning and teaching initiative being implemented as part of the current reform of higher education, a greatly enhanced national Australian Awards for University Teaching scheme which, from 2006, will comprise 250 annual teaching awards.

The third major initiative in learning and teaching is establishment of the Learning and Teaching Performance Fund, a scheme aimed at rewarding those universities that best demonstrate excellence in learning and teaching. The amount of funding associated with the scheme is Aus. $250 million over three years, which will be given to a small number of universities according to their performance against seven indicators related to learning and teaching. Interestingly, publication of the quantitative scores on which the funding will be based, derived from combining the performance indicator data, has given rise to a de facto ranking of Australian universities as to their learning and teaching performance. The result is that some older and highly prestigious universities have been ranked near the bottom and there has been considerable national debate focused on how we should assess learning and teaching outcomes at the institutional level.

Perhaps the most significant feature of the Learning and Teaching Performance Fund is that to be eligible for funding a university had to first satisfy the Commonwealth government that it had met a series of requirements considered to represent minimum standards for learning and teaching:

- A current and recent institutional learning and teaching plan or strategy
- Evidence of systematic support for professional development in learning and teaching for sessional and full-time academic staff
- Documentation on academic probation and promotions policies and practices that indicate staff are required to provide evidence of their effectiveness as a teacher
- Evidence of systematic student evaluation of teaching and subjects that inform probation and promotion decisions for academic positions

Given the high level of funding associated with the Learning and Teaching Performance Fund, not surprisingly all universities put considerable effort into meeting these requirements even though this did not, by itself, result in any funding. Thus, the Commonwealth government was able, through this eligibility process, to bring about significant changes aimed at enhancing learning and teaching across all universities.

Future Directions

Amid so much major structural reform, it is difficult to predict the direction Australian higher education is likely to take in the immediate future. A key feature of the current reform agenda is deregulation of the higher education sector and creation of an environment where universities are more responsive to outside pressure. However, whether the concerns of students and their families about the costs of higher education, insistence on more relevant and practical curricula from employers, demands for more flexible access to higher education, or competition from nonuniversity providers will dominate future developments remains to be seen.

What is clear, however, is that these issues will be played out in a uniquely Australian context. Built on a strong English and Scottish tradition of public universities, Australian higher education is influenced by developments in North America, and also—because of its geographic position—increasingly responsive to its Asian neighbors. Deepening engagement with the rapid social and economic developments occurring in the Asian region while retaining strong connections with Europe and North America offers the potential of creating in Australia a unique international approach to higher education that will better meet the needs of learners in the future.

References

Australian Vice-Chancellors' Committee (AVCC). *Key Statistics on Higher Education.* Canberra: Australian Vice-Chancellors' Committee, 2005.

Department of Education, Training, and Youth Affairs (DETYA). *The Australian Higher Education Quality Assurance Framework.* Canberra: Commonwealth of Australia, 2000.

Department of Employment, Education, and Training (DEET). *National Report on Australia's Higher Education Sector.* Canberra: Australian Government Publishing Service, 1993.

Higher Education Council (HEC). *Higher Education, Achieving Quality.* Canberra: Australian Government Publishing Service, 1992.

Nelson, B. *Higher Education at the Crossroads.* Canberra: Department of Education, Science, and Training, Commonwealth of Australia, 2002.

Nelson, B. *Higher Education: Report for the 2004 to 2006 Triennium.* Canberra: Department of Education, Science, and Training, Commonwealth of Australia, 2004.

Nelson, B. *Higher Education Report 2004–05.* Canberra: Department of Education, Science, and Training, Commonwealth of Australia, 2005.

JOHN M. DEARN is pro vice-chancellor (academic) and vice president at the University of Canberra in Australia, where he is responsible for academic strategy and policy development, teaching strategies, and the quality of educational outcomes.

5

In the United Kingdom both institutions and government have taken initiatives to enhance student learning on a broad scale.

Quest for Quality: The UK Experience

Brenda M. Smith

This chapter explores how higher education in the United Kingdom ensures the quality of its programs and encourages initiatives to enhance the student learning experience. First, I describe how higher education institutions (HEIs) are funded and supported. Second, I look at how standards and quality of provision are developed and maintained. Third, I discuss government initiatives, specifically in England, that fund strategies aimed at enhancement of student learning on a broad scale. Finally, I explore some of the challenges that lie ahead.

Funding and Support for HEIs

The United Kingdom has 164 universities, of which 130 are in England, 20 in Scotland, 12 in Wales, and 2 in Northern Ireland. The increase in the number of universities was as a result of polytechnics being granted university status in 1992. The number of universities continues to grow as selected colleges attain university status. Universities of the four countries of the United Kingdom (England, Northern Ireland, Scotland, and Wales) are funded by their respective funding councils, student tuition fees, and income derived from donations.

From autumn 2006, annual tuition fees at universities in England, currently a flat rate of £1,150, will vary from nothing to £3,000 depending on the institution. To be allowed to increase tuition fees, universities must invest some of the extra income in attracting students from low-income groups. Most institutions are setting aside 20 to 30 percent of their additional

NEW DIRECTIONS FOR HIGHER EDUCATION, no. 133, Spring 2006 © Wiley Periodicals, Inc.
Published online in Wiley InterScience (www.interscience.wiley.com) • DOI: 10.1002/he.204

fee income for bursaries and other forms of financial support. Unlike now, students will no longer have to pay up front while at university, unless they choose to. Instead fees will be covered by a loan, repayable by graduates once their annual income passes £15,000. Some fear that this runs counter to the widening participation target for 50 percent of all seventeen-to-thirty-year-olds to have experienced higher education by 2010. The current figure stands at 44 percent in England and 50 percent in Scotland. However, the most advantaged 20 percent of young people are as much as six times more likely to enter higher education than the most disadvantaged 20 percent.

Space allows discussion of only the largest funding council, the Higher Education Funding Council for England (HEFCE), which was set up by the UK government in 1992 as a "nondepartmental public body," with distinct statutory duties free from political control. HEFCE supports four main strategic aims:

1. Enhancing excellence in learning and teaching
2. Widening participation and fair access
3. Enhancing excellence in research
4. Enhancing the contribution of higher education to the economy and society

The first, enhancing excellence in learning and teaching, focuses on the student, where HEFCE will "seek to ensure that every student benefits from a good education through the highest quality of teaching and the best possible facilities and opportunities to learn" (HEFCE, 2004–05, p. 5a).

This is achieved by HEFCE in a variety of ways, but by far the largest funded initiative for enhancing learning and teaching was launched in 2004–05 for institutions to bid for Centres of Excellence in Teaching and Learning (CETL). £315 million is being allocated over five years to fund seventy-four centers, following a two-stage bidding process. Each CETL will receive recurrent funding, ranging from £200,000 to £500,000 per annum for five years, and a capital sum ranging from £0.8 million to £2 million.

The purpose of CETLs is to enhance student learning for a specified number of students that the institution has identified and to recognize and reward staff. Recognition for staff could take the form of enhanced pay or an offer of promotion to a senior position or professorship. Most CETLs are built around a specific discipline, such as engineering or medicine, or a theme such as assessment, developing creativity, or clinical and communication skills. A full list of the CETLs and their foci can be accessed at www.hefce.ac.uk/learning/TInits/cetl.

Each CETL is led by a director and usually centrally based or within a department. Funding could pay for additional staff or consultants, which enables for example teaching smaller groups, employing external expertise, linking with professional practitioners, or freeing up staff time to develop curriculum materials. In addition, the funding could update equipment, renovate existing space, or build facilities. The CETLs are being encouraged to engage in pedagogic research, especially to focus on garnering evidence that the CETL has enhanced student learning. A key role and challenge for each CETL will be to disseminate effective practices within and across institutions.

A significant new UK organization is the Higher Education Academy, which began operating in 2004. It is an independent body ("owned" not by the government but by the sector's representative bodies, Universities UK and the Standing Conference of Principals) and funded through the UK funding bodies and UK universities. It was formed from amalgamation of three former organizations: the Learning and Teaching Support Network (LTSN), the Institute for Learning and Teaching in Higher Education (ILTHE), and the National Coordination Team (NCT). The role of the academy is to work with universities and colleges, discipline groups, and individual staff to help them deliver the best possible learning experience for students.

The academy supports institutions in their strategic plans in relation to learning and teaching, leads research and evaluation to improve the quality of student experience, and assists professional development and recognition of all staff in higher education (the latter is achieved also by accrediting institutional educational development programs). As a result of recommendations of a White Paper (1999), it is now mandatory for all new university teaching staff without recent or relevant teaching experience to attend one of these institutional programs. In addition, we now have a consultation document on a standards framework for staff that teaches and supports learning. Developed by the Higher Education sector, the proposed framework "seeks to maintain institutional ownership of the criteria by which the standards are met at the same time as providing a single overarching structure for the professional development of staff who support student learning" (Higher Education Academy, 2005, p. 1).

Key features of the academy are its twenty-four subject centers, located within relevant subject departments and hosted by HEIs. The subject focus recognizes that for many higher education staff, most networking and exchange of learning, teaching, and assessment practice takes place at this level.

The core activities of each subject center include collation of information, training opportunities, networks, advice on technology, and up-to-date information and resources. This information can be accessed at www. heacademy.ac.uk. Although the Higher Education Academy is still in its inception, it clearly has a major role in terms of bringing coherence and coordination to the United Kingdom with respect to effective learning and teaching practices. However, the role of the academy is focused on enhancing quality and does not include monitoring quality and standards, which is carried out by the Quality Assurance Agency (QAA).

Maintaining Standards and Quality

Institutions need to set procedures; maintain and review their own quality and standards; and furnish relevant information for students, employers, and the general public. This public accountability is carried out by the QAA (www.qaa.ac.uk) and varies among the four UK countries. Here I discuss England and Scotland.

In 1994 QAA set out to review all subject provisions over a five-year time scale in every university in England. This process was based on a self-evaluation document evaluated by a team of assessors/reviewers visiting institutions on a subject by subject basis. At the end of the visit, oral feedback was given and departments received a score based on six core aspects of provision:

- Curriculum design, content, and organization
- Teaching, learning, and assessment
- Student progression and achievement
- Student support and guidance
- Learning resources
- Quality management and enhancement

Disadvantages of this system included the cost in time and human and material resources. Departments spent twelve months or more preparing for the visit—a huge burden that deflected attention away from other aspects of university life, especially curriculum innovation. The process not only generated a paper mountain, which many saw as voluminous statistics, but also created high stress and led to the inevitable national league tables in which universities were ranked according to the scores obtained from the QAA visit.

However, there were also many advantages of the system. It yielded evidence that standards were high and offered an impetus for institutions to give more attention to the quality of their teaching. The student voice was heard, and senior managers took the process seriously. It also gave a focus to institutional staff development, which previously was not highlighted, though "all academics indicated that being an assessor had exerted a positive influence on their educational practices" (McDowell and Colling, 1997, p. 9a). The system promoted more rigorous internal quality assessment (QA) procedures, often leading to "reshaping the institutional policies and procedures" (p. 8b). Most important, it raised the profile of learning and teaching in all institutions.

In 2001, the arrangement for ensuring the quality of teaching and the standards of awards in HEIs were revised (HEFCE, 2001). Continuation audits and subject review by the QAA were replaced with the quality assurance framework (QAF). This comprises institutional audits by QAA, collaborative provision audits, and publication of information about quality and standards through the Teaching Quality Information (TQI) Website. QAF includes the results of the first National Student Survey (NSS), to be discussed later.

The revised quality assurance processes were implemented through a transitional cycle between 2002 and 2005, in which each HEI received one or more developmental engagements and an institutional audit. A review in 2004 focused on the impacts, benefits, and costs of the QAA institutional review. Recommendations included streamlining the system; allowing institutions to share good practice; and making it possible for professional, statutory, and regulatory bodies to work more closely with QAA. Overall, "it is clear that there has been very significant reduction in the cost of QA for the sector since this issue was first raised in 2000. All the main government-funded QA processes we have reviewed have a specific purpose and deliver benefits" (HEFCE, 2005b, p. 25).

Scrutiny of quality in Scotland has, by contrast, taken a more radical stance. Over the past decade, the higher education sector in Scotland has participated in a range of initiatives in external assurance of quality and standards. The outcomes of these activities demonstrate that in general Scottish higher education institutions had in place effective quality management systems relating to the experience of students and the standards of their awards, and that subject provision experienced by students was highly satisfactory or better.

Following consultation by the Scottish Higher Education Funding Council (SHEFC), a more explicit focus was given to enhancement of the learning experience of students. The agenda was developed as a four-way partnership of SHEFC, the QAA in Scotland, Universities Scotland, and the National Union of Students, Scotland; it consists of five interrelated aspects:

1. Internal review at the subject level
2. Public information set
3. Effective involvement of students in quality management
4. Enhancement-led institutional review
5. Enhancement themes

A key part of this model is the enhancement themes, developed by the steering committees that act as vehicles for planning and implementing a program of work for each theme. A strategic plan is developed, with public events including conferences, workshops, and expert consultations. In this way, the enhancement themes aim to engage and interact with the whole academic community. The themes enable Scottish higher education provision to be benchmarked against global best practice, with the work being informed by international expertise and exemplars of good practice. The published outcomes of the enhancement themes work are a growing international resource (www.enhancementthemes.ac.uk).

Enhancement work in Scotland is particularly keen to involve students. Indeed a notable change over the last five to ten years across the United Kingdom has been active involvement of students and real interest in listening to their views. Students now have more say in improving the quality of courses and have better information to help them choose what suits them.

Two new developments enabling this to happen are a new TQI Website and the first-ever comprehensive national student survey giving feedback on the quality of their courses. Key statistics and reports on every course in England have been available since the summer of 2005. The Web site will include qualitative data on students' entry qualifications, progression, completion of awards, and subsequent employment, together with qualitative reports provided by the institutions themselves. Information about the student survey and the outcomes can be accessed at http://www.hefce.ac.uk/learning/nss.

Fazackerley and Shepherd (2005, p. 1) "urged Vice chancellors to take a hard look at the performance of their departments." The survey also revealed that many "un-fashionable" universities are rated the best in the country by their undergraduates. It is to be hoped that institutions use the information constructively to improve individual programs and other structures that lead to enhancement of the student learning experience.

Thus the last twenty years have seen increased public accountability, changes from quality management to quality enhancement, more structured and systematic institutional approaches to quality enhancement, acknowledgment of staff development as a key driver for change, and greater attention to the voice of students. At the same time, there is a genuine intention to disseminate and embed effective practices across UK higher education.

Government Initiatives

Support for learning and teaching has not suddenly emerged but has been part of a continuous program of initiatives funded by several agencies. This section highlights a number of these initiatives, putting them in a historical context up to the present day.

The first externally funded initiative was the Enterprise in Higher Education (EHE) program in 1987, designed to encourage development of qualities of enterprise among those seeking higher education qualifications. Following EHE, the context of higher education started to change; modularization and semesterization became accepted by staff in institutions. One consequence of this was that programs and courses were split into smaller units called modules, which were generally delivered over a semester. Many staff felt that what they once delivered over a whole academic year now had to be compressed into a semester; skills development became less of a focus and a number of the innovations lay dormant.

Following the EHE program was the Computers in Teaching Initiative (CTI) in 1989 and the Teaching and Learning Technology Programme (TLTP) in 1992. Both were aimed at making teaching and learning more productive and efficient by harnessing modern technology. However, these initiatives tended to be technology-led, rather than pedagogically focused.

In 2005 HEFCE launched an e-learning strategy: "E-learning has been criticised for being technology led, with a focus on providing materials, but has relatively recently focused more on the learner and enabling students and other users to develop more independence in learning and to share resources. This change matches developments in pedagogy and the increasing need to support diversity and flexibility in higher education" (HEFCE, 2005a, p. 4). It is to be hoped that this initiative will have a greater focus on student learning.

The turning point in terms of more coherent thinking on learning and teaching was the influential Dearing Report (NCIHE, 1997), advising on the long-term development of higher education. As a consequence of this report and its fifty recommendations, HEFCE undertook an extensive consultation (HEFCE, 1998) with the outcome focusing on five key themes: encouragement and reward, coordination and collaboration, disseminating and embedding good practice, research and innovation, and building capacity for change.

To deliver this strategy, the HEFCE established a Teaching Quality Enhancement Fund (TQEF). One of its strengths was a multifunctional fund that took a three-pronged approach to enhancement, focusing on the three levels of institution, subject, and individual.

At the institutional level, higher education institutions now produce "learning and teaching strategies" to ensure a strategic vision of how they will identify and address learning and teaching issues. In England and Wales, institutions are required to produce learning and teaching strategies along with operational plans. Resources relating to the size of the university are currently offered to support institutions in addressing the issues they identify.

The second level, which focused on the subject element, had two components. The first is a development tool, the Fund for the Development of Teaching and Learning (FDTL), which aims to encourage and fund innovation on the basis of excellence as defined by the subject review process of the QAA. The second component was the Learning and Teaching Support Network (LTSN), which is now part of the Higher Education Academy.

Invitations to bid for FDTL funding followed from a subject review of specific discipline areas (HEFCE, 1995). To date five phases of funding have been allocated. The key to the program is that funding support is given to those subject providers who performed well in subject review, with the aim of more widely disseminating good practice. Thus FDTL was the first form of funding to be seen as explicitly rewarding excellence. A National Coordination Team supported the FDTL program in lending essential education development expertise and gave support in planning, disseminating, and sharing effective practices. This work is now being carried out by the Higher Education Academy.

The third level of support was the individual, via the National Teaching Fellowship Scheme (2006), which rewards and recognizes individual staff to begin generating the kudos already associated with academic staff undertaking nationally and internationally excellent research activity. Since 2000, twenty National Teaching Fellowships have been awarded each year on the basis of outstanding work in the development of learning and teaching. This was extended to make fifty awards per year to include "rising stars" and academic support staff. For 2006, the new scheme comprises two strands, Individual National Teaching Fellowship Reward and Project Awards (www.ntfs.ac.uk/).

In conclusion, it is difficult to evaluate the long-term impact of these initiatives in terms of their effectiveness and sustainability. Influences on practice come from many directions, and isolating one factor against others is impossible. What can be said, however, is that these initiatives contribute to a climate of support for learning and teaching. Teaching is now on the agenda, which is very different from ten or fifteen years ago.

Parallel to these initiatives comes increasing pressure on staff to also achieve excellence in research. The Research Assessment Exercise (RAE) in the United Kingdom has led to tremendous pressure. The RAE is "a series of exercises conducted nationally to assess the quality of UK research and to inform the selective distribution of public funds for research by the four UK higher education funding bodies. RAE 2008 will provide quality profiles for research across all disciplines. Submissions from institutions will be assessed by experts in some 70 units of assessment." Details are at www.rae.ac.uk/.

Many staff have felt the RAE to be detrimental to learning and teaching in that recognition and reward come only from research. As Elton (2005) points out, "Since the RAE is so important it gets time preference everywhere. It's difficult to find time to do anything else other than straight teaching. Pedagogic research is only going to be by the back door." However, the newly launched CETLs may be one way to redress the balance. In addition, a longstanding debate is gaining momentum as to how the teaching-research nexus can be more fruitful rather than competitive in terms of staff time (Jenkins, 2004). In addition, there is a groundswell to encourage developing the scholarship of learning and teaching to be equally valued and resourced as the RAE. In September 2005, HEFCE announced additional funding to support teaching informed research for 2006–2008, allocated in inverse proportion to an institution's research funding. This is a positive step forward for student learning and will be welcomed by many.

NEW DIRECTIONS FOR HIGHER EDUCATION • DOI 10.1002/he

Support for enhancing learning and teaching has developed and increased over the last twenty years, with funding coming from a variety of sources, particularly internal allocation of funds on the part of universities. This is evidenced by almost all universities having named centers to support learning and teaching. A recent development has been moves to link these central units at the departmental level, resulting in staff being appointed as teaching fellows or learning and teaching coordinators, but based in the department. This enables a more focused approach to the differing needs of the various disciplines. However, the very real challenge for the central unit is not only to initiate development but also to disseminate effective learning and teaching practices within and across institutions. There is also a need to link with those external organizations, such as the Higher Education Academy, that can support them in this work.

These initiatives have led to a great deal of curriculum innovation, notably peer and self-assessment, distance learning courses, small group work, and students being encouraged to take on more responsibility for their own learning. There is an emphasis on preparing students for lifelong learning, including developing a range of skills desired by employers such as showing initiative and working in teams.

However, all these developments have come at a cost. There is enormous pressure on staff to be successful in teaching, research, and administration, which leads to a high level of stress. These changes have also come at a time of increased student numbers, reduced resources, growing diversity among students, and external scrutiny to enhance standards and the quality of teaching and greater public accountability.

Although funding to support learning and teaching initiatives is on the increase, funding by itself will not achieve enhancement of student learning. Staff need time and appropriate support structures to enable development and embedding of these effective practices if the student learning experience is to be enhanced. Senior staff need training and support to cope with the conflicting demands of being a senior manager; they are often caught on the treadmill of funding, policy initiatives, and concern for reputation. In addition, more research is needed to explore how dissemination of effective practices can be achieved within and across institutions, as well as integrated and sustained once the funding comes to an end.

References

Brennan, J., Frederiks, M., and Shah, T. "Improving the Quality of Education: The Impact of Quality Assessment on Institutions." Bristol: Higher Education Funding Council for England, 1997.

Elton, L. "Teaching Status Scrutinised." *Times Educational Supplement,* May 20, 2005, p. 2.

Fazackerley, A., and Shepherd, J. "Student Poll Puts Staff Under Pressure." *Times Educational Supplement,* Sept. 23, 2005, p. 1.

Higher Education Academy. "A Standards Framework for Teaching and Supporting Student Learning in Higher Education. Consultation Document." York: Higher Education Academy, 2005. http://www.heacademy.ac.uk/standards framework.

Higher Education Funding Council for England. "Fund for the Development of Teaching and Learning." No. 29/95. 1995. http://www.hefce.ac.uk/pubs/hefce/1995/c29_95.htm.

Higher Education Funding Council for England. "Learning and Teaching: Strategy and Funding Proposals." No. 98/40. Bristol: HEFCE, 1998. http://www.hefce.ac.uk/pubs/hefce/1998/98_40.htm.

Higher Education Funding Council for England. "Quality Assurance in Higher Education—Proposals for Consultation." No. 01/45. Bristol: HEFCE, July 2001. http://www.hefce.ac.uk/pubs/hefce/2001/01_45.htm.

Higher Education Funding Council for England. "Changing the Landscape of Higher Education." Annual review. Bristol: HEFCE, 2004–05. http://www.hefce.ac.uk/pubs/hefce/2005/annrev.

Higher Education Funding Council for England. "HEFCE Strategy for E-learning." No. 2005/12. Bristol: HEFCE, 2005a. http://www.hefce.ac.uk/pubs/hefce/2005/05_12.

Higher Education Funding Council for England. "Review of the Quality Assurance Framework. Phase One Outcomes." 2005/35. Bristol: HEFCE, 2005b. http://www.hefce.ac.uk/pubs/hefce/2005/05_35.

Jenkins, A. "A Guide to the Research Evidence on Teaching-Research Relations." York: Higher Education Academy, 2004. http://www.heacademy.ac.uk/resources.asp?process=full_record&section=generic&id=383.

McDowell, L., and Colling, C. "Improving the Quality of Education: The Impacts of Subject Specialist Assessor Experience." Bristol: Higher Education Funding Council for England, 1997. http://www.hefce.ac.uk/pubs/hefce/1997/M15_97.htm.

National Committee of Inquiry into Higher Education (NCIHE). *Higher Education in the Learning Society: Report of the National Committee (The Dearing Report).* London: National Committee of Inquiry into Higher Education and the Learning Society, 1997.

National Teaching Fellowship Scheme. 2006. http://www.heacademy.ac.uk/ntfs.htm.

"White Paper: Learning to Succeed—A New Framework for Post 16 Learning." 1999. http://www.hefce.ac.uk/learning/ltos.htm.

BRENDA M. SMITH *is associate director with the Higher Education Academy. She has acted as a consultant in fifteen countries.*

6

*Traditionally, the higher education sector in Germany
has been research oriented. During their studies of ten to
thirteen semesters, students have had close contact with
research and have been motivated by new findings they
have discovered themselves. Introducing a bachelor's- and
master's-style structure into the current system means in
many cases losing this close contact at the bachelor's
level. Only a few programs developed professionally
maintain this link.*

German Policy Perspectives on Enhancing the Quality of Student Learning by University Teaching

Wolff-Dietrich Webler

To explain the higher education (HE) system in Germany from macro to micro structure, it must be realized that Germany consists of sixteen federal states, which have sovereignty in cultural affairs. The HE system is divided into traditional universities and *Fachhochschulen* (universities of applied sciences). The first group is more oriented toward fundamental research; it has the task of developing the scholarly disciplines. The second group has the task of producing applied research, making close connections with industry to enable more technology transfer, and offering study programs with a more vocational profile (binary system). Almost all of the traditional universities are state institutions; only among the Fachhochschulen are there many "private" institutions (which in many cases means they are run by churches, mainly for social professions). There is a federal HE Framework Law; this is because the German constitution asks for all areas to be developed to a similar level, which means in regard to education that mobility of students and families among the states must be ensured. The HE system consists of one hundred traditional universities (average number of students twenty thousand) and 150 universities of applied sciences (average number of students eight to fifteen thousand). It is perhaps a specialty of Germany (and can also be observed in Canada) that until now there has been no elitist sector. All the traditional universities on the one hand and all Fachhochschulen on the other are expected to be of equal quality (local differences may occur over

time and because of staff changes), although this belief has been weakened as rankings have shown there are more differences between universities than was known before. There is mild competition among the federal states in educational affairs, a competition from which the universities benefit, because the states want to demonstrate their power to finance a very good university. All universities, particularly the traditional ones, undertake research as part of their tasks; however, differences exist mainly in the level of funding. Some universities define themselves as research universities more than others do.

Universities in Germany are autonomous in academic affairs. In the federal state of Lower Saxony (Niedersachsen), there is a law that allows universities to become foundations, which gives them full autonomy. Each university can individually decide whether or not to pursue this path. The state equips the university with a "treasure" as capital with which to start. These universities organize themselves, build up their own budget, and appoint professors on their own. In Germany, in contrast to other HE systems, professors are appointed for life. The reasoning behind this is to make them more independent of the state and to maintain the scholarly freedom to teach.

The main indicator for a successful career inside academia is research and publications. Only gradually does teaching become more important. This demonstration of productivity is needed because traditionally in Germany the tenure track has not existed. Additionally, appointment to a professorship in one's own university is forbidden (with few exceptions). Scholars are forced to be successful in a university other than the one in which they did their initial studies and took their first professional steps. This is why the universities are roughly equal in quality (apart from a few exceptions where a special center of excellence has been established locally). Young scholars show high mobility between universities until they achieve a full professorship. Afterward, in many cases they stay for the remainder of their career, which makes staff turnover slow.

Controlling or Supporting the Quality of Learning and Teaching

Every department has to present a teaching report relating to a range of indicators (mainly set by the ministry) to the top of the university (rectorat, or presidency, and senate) every one or two years (depending on the state). Indicators are the number of applicants, new students, graduates, and successfully absolved exams during and at the end of the degree. According to HE law of some federal states, parts of the report could include

• Measures taken to maintain a high standard of teaching
• Counseling of students
• Adherence to the prescribed period of study
• Feedback from the students about the quality of teaching

NEW DIRECTIONS FOR HIGHER EDUCATION • DOI 10.1002/he

• Responses of the teaching staff to the results from the student feedback and about evaluations

This report has to show measures to improve weaknesses; steps forward are to be shown in subsequent reports. This report must include the results of the evaluation of courses (student rating or more).

As an additional means to ensure or improve quality, there is accreditation of study programs in the framing concept of Bologna (presented later in this chapter). This accreditation system was established during the last six years. It consists of the German Accreditation Board, which approves accreditation agencies (six at the moment) that organize the individual procedures. The board has defined a framework of rules for accreditation of study programs, and the agencies have formulated some additional rules. The universities prepare their applications, for one or a number of programs (cluster accreditation), to be accredited.

Funding for Institutions Dependent on Quality of Learning and Teaching

Over the last ten years, success-oriented budgeting of HE institutions (HEI) has been introduced step by step. The budget is disseminated among the HEI of a certain federal state according to various indicators (in Northrhine-Westfalia, they consist of the amount of external funds for research and development (those bringing in more extramural or external funds receive more money from the state), the number of students within their prescribed period of study (the time within which students should finish their studies), the number of students who have passed their last examination, and the number of doctoral degrees awarded per year. Improving the number of students within the regular time of studies and reducing the number of students overrunning has yielded additional measures to improve the quality of learning and teaching (more transparent information, better counseling, introduction of tutorial systems, more interest in educational development).

Unusually, although studies in Germany are generally free of tuition (at least for the first degree, such as bachelor's programs), in some federal states students who exceed a certain number of semesters in their studies have to pay study fees. According to a formula of dissemination, the universities get this money back, but it is designated to be spent only on improvement of teaching and learning.

Impact of Policy Documents on Approaches Taken to Enhance Learning and Teaching

The Bologna concept of HE is the document that has influenced European HE most deeply in recent years. It started in 1998 with a declaration (the Bologna Declaration) by a group of member states of the European Union

(EU) at a meeting in Bologna, Italy. In the meantime, all European states (not just EU members) declared that they were ready to form a common area of HE policy. The declaration consists of several points:

- A study system with three degree levels (bachelor's, master's, and doc-toral studies) is to be created.
- The first degree levels have a combined length of ten semesters (six plus four, seven plus three, or eight plus two).
- Independent studies of students should be strengthened.
- Studies are structured in modules, which combine courses and indepen-dent study around a common idea, theme, or notion.
- With this structure, mobility should be supported (students can easily collect complete modules and credit points, enabling them to study one or two semesters in another country).
- Study programs should have an international, especially European, com-ponent (to support intercultural competencies).
- Modules should be described more in terms of the competencies to be achieved by the students than by the content to be taught (learning out-come and output driven rather than input driven).
- Each module (instead of every course) ends with a test.
- Accordingly, it is not the lessons taught (counted in hours) but the work-load on the students' side that is the basis for curriculum planning.
- The acceptable workload for students is nine hundred hours per semes-ter.
- There are both a quantitative (credit points) and a qualitative system (marks), which work in parallel, to document the students' success in their studies.
- Students get one credit point for thirty hours of workload.
- The study programs should ensure employability.
- All of these measures should be implemented by 2010.

Consequently, many European traditions in HE will have to be har-monized. In Germany, this political decision has caused skeptical reactions inside the universities, because the difference from the traditional struc-ture of study programs is dramatic (Webler, 2005a). The Bologna concept is highly controversial because of its impression that the traditional, highly esteemed, German way to educate excellent young scholars will be destroyed by this division into bachelor's and master's studies (Webler 2004). American friends and colleagues of the author who completed part of their own studies at German universities shouted, "You (collectively) are silly," when told that Germany would introduce the bachelor's and master's structure. "Do you have any idea of the mountain of problems you are facing by introducing this system?"

NEW DIRECTIONS FOR HIGHER EDUCATION • DOI 10.1002/he

Until now, scholarly study programs at universities have been eight to ten semesters. Many traditional teachers at universities were convinced that anything shorter than this would not be enough time for careful and solid preparation for professional work. A number of teachers in HE in Germany still hope the plan will be cancelled, or at least modified. Disciplines such as psychology and electrical engineering have not even started reforming their curricula, but many others have begun the process. In many cases there are problems with the newly created bachelor's curricula. First of all, not every teacher in HE is well enough informed about the details of the Bologna concept. Hardly anyone has been professionally prepared to develop curricula. Approaches for better learning and the central role of learning in comparison to teaching ("the shift from teaching to learning") as a way to make studies more effective have not yet arrived in many departments. Instead, teacher- and content-centered styles of teaching are practiced. To justify their claims on study programs and resources, they try to teach the same amount of content in six semesters as was taught before in eight semesters. The consequences are too many lessons and too much learning like school pupils. Furthermore, teachers are not used to thinking in terms of competencies to be achieved by the students, nor in terms of learning outcomes, but rather in terms of teaching input. Modules are described and taught not in competencies but in traditional content-oriented titles. The accreditation procedures, created to control quality and harmony with the Bologna concept, fail in the majority of cases because the peers are generally colleagues from the same discipline who have had no further training for their new task.

Many bachelor's study programs have begun. In a number of cases, students have far too much work, because the estimated workload was not realistic. Students are mainly preparing for tests (a surface approach to learning) instead of learning so as to gain deeper understanding of the subject and connections to a theme (deep learning approach). Teachers are horrified by the large amount of test correction required as their homework. So, at the moment too many curricula are missing the idea of the Bologna concept, and teachers and students are hardly able to deal with the consequences. In this situation, teachers are more open to reform and professional development in teaching and learning.

In some federal states, it is a legal role of the university to offer workshops for academic staff and educational development as a contribution to the quality of teaching and learning. Hence teachers have a chance to improve their ability to offer learning opportunities to students by better teaching.

The last reform introduced success-oriented components into the salary system. In the future, teachers will get extra money for successful work (research, teaching, and perhaps academic self-government). Indicators will be developed in the near future.

NEW DIRECTIONS FOR HIGHER EDUCATION • DOI 10.1002/he

Inquiries into Learning and Teaching and Professional Development Projects

In Germany a network of institutes are conducting research on HE ranging from studies in science to studies in learning and teaching. The latter are running projects on professional development. In differing contexts, there are inquiries (some of which are quite extensive) into learning and teaching. The main institutes in this field in recent years have been the *Arbeitsgruppe Hochschulforschung* (Workgroup Research on HE) at the University of Konstanz, the *Hochschul-Informationssystem* (HIS) in Hannover, and the *Interdisziplinäres Zentrum für Hochschuldidaktik"* (IZHD or Interdisciplinary Center for Academic Staff and Educational Development) at the University of Bielefeld; they are now followed by the *Institut für Wissenschafts- und Bildungsforschung Bielefeld* (IWBB, Bielefeld Institute for Research on Science and Education), the *Bayerisches Staatsinstitut für Hochschulforschung und Hochschulplanung* (Bavarian State Institute for Research and Planning in HE) in Munich, the *Wissenschaftliches Zentrum für Berufs- und Hochschulforschung* (Scholarly Center for Research on HE and Work) at the University of Kassel, the *Institut für Hochschulforschung* (Institute for Research on HE) at the University of Halle/Wittenberg, and especially for professional development projects the IWBB and the *Hochschuldidaktisches Zentrum* (Center for Academic Staff and Educational Development) at the University of Dortmund.

Associations and Initiatives Aimed at Enhancing Learning and Teaching

Since the end of the 1960s, the German Society for Educational Development in HE (*Arbeitsgemeinschaft für Hochschuldidaktik,* or AHD) has supported initiatives to improve teaching and learning in HE through a journal, books, articles, conferences, and workshops. The members are teachers, trainers, and students.

In the first half of the 1970s the two Interdisciplinary Centers for Academic Staff and Educational Development at the universities of Hamburg and Bielefeld (with the same name: *Interdisziplinäres Zentrum für Hochschuldidaktik,* or IZHD) started workshops for staff and educational development, followed by other centers at the Free University and the Technical University at Berlin and the Center for Staff and Educational Development at the University of Dortmund. In the federal state of Lower Saxony (Niedersachsen), the center at the Technical University at Brunswick started such a program in the 1990s and has offered workshops to all HEIs in this state.

In 2000, the federal state of Baden-Württemberg, together with the universities, established the nationwide Center for Academic and Staff Development. This was started as an initiative to establish a regional infrastructure for its nine universities to offer a program for young scholars to achieve

NEW DIRECTIONS FOR HIGHER EDUCATION • DOI 10.1002/he

teaching competence in a curriculum of two hundred contact hours of workshops, reflective writing, experimental teaching, and so on. Of all initiatives in Germany, this center is the most effective. More than twelve hundred people have taken part in this training in the last two years. In 2003, the Parliament of Bayern (Bavaria) decided to found a structure similar to Baden-Württemberg's program with 120 hours of contact, making it obligatory for every teacher in HE to take part.

Other networks are quite successful too, especially in Northern Germany. The three centers and four workgroups for Staff and Educational Development of Northrhine-Westphalia have agreed to a similar program, which has been offered to all universities in the state for the last five years. The author has developed a similar program and first introduced it at the University of Osnabrück. Since then, a network was founded among three universities, and the program is run at the universities of Bremen and Oldenburg as well. In addition, many local groups of young teachers have initiated workshops on learning and teaching using external moderators, depending on whether they can get funding from the department or the university. Normally, such workshops take place only once or twice a year. Individual institutions such as the University of Kassel have developed their own training program to achieve teaching competencies. Kassel has a structure of 120 contact hours for a program leading to a certificate for teaching ability. Thus initiatives exist at many universities, despite the fact that teaching abilities are still not of high importance in appointment procedures. These teachers, especially young ones, feel responsible for students and want to be trained—despite the fact that this has little relevance for their own scholarly career.

Main Challenges to Enhance Learning and Teaching

There are two main reasons that enhancing learning and teaching has become so important in Germany. One is that many study programs have a high dropout rate: (the range is from 7 percent (for example, in economics dual studies or sandwich programs combining work with university education) to 84 percent (such as in German studies). Public and political pressure is the main cause for improvement here. The second reason consists of the new Bologna structure of study programs, which generates urgent challenges to enhance learning and teaching. Orientation is needed in selection of modules (if there is any decision making left for students) and preparation of decisions connected with proceeding from a bachelor's to a master's program.

Recent Developments

Reintroduction of study fees at German universities (such fees were stopped in the beginning of the 1970s) is under way in the federal states and is supported by the argument that they will improve the quality of teaching. The

New Directions for Higher Education • DOI 10.1002/he

author, who studied under such conditions during the late 1960s (with no effect on the quality of teaching), cannot see any connection between the two (quality and fees), especially because the teacher will not get any extra money from the tuition fees.

Some universities tend to blame the students for not being successful enough in their studies. Therefore they tend to select their students before enrollment, hoping that the match between students and study offerings will improve and they can avoid having to improve their study offerings. Universities are now allowed to introduce this method for 20 percent of their new students (it will soon increase to 40 percent). Many problems and questions arise from this procedure: How valid is the prognosis connected with the procedure? How severe is the impact on further social discrimination? How time-consuming is this procedure? and so on.

Universities are developing their own system of quality assurance for their learning and teaching offerings. Parts of it were simply obligatory owing to changes in legislation, such as student rating of lectures and seminars, while other parts became attractive thanks to a system of success-oriented budgeting of universities. Within a range of indicators for success, one stood out clearly: student success rate within the mandatory time-frame of the specific study program. Hence departments became interested in the success of their students. In many universities, evaluation programs are run that include the questioning of students and teachers as a first step and peer review of the results as a second step.

The main effort for enhancing quality in the last five years consisted of introducing a system of accreditation of study programs by peer review. Framed and coordinated by the German Accreditation Council, agencies are running accreditation procedures for each study program, done by peers. Such study programs are accepted only for five years, after which reaccreditation is required. This is connected with a large amount of empirical data about experience with the program. Decision making is directly dependent on the quality of the reviewers and consequently there is much debate on the procedure, asking for at least some training of the reviewers.

Learning and Teaching in Research-Oriented Institutions

Do differing degrees of support for learning and teaching, especially various institutional strategies, depend on research orientation? The *Fachhochschulen* are more teaching-oriented than the majority of the traditional research-oriented universities. Furthermore, the more research-oriented among the traditional universities are generally less interested in learning and teaching. Yet it seems that openness to questions of learning and teaching is more a question of the disciplinary culture than of research orientation. This has something to do with the pragmatism in these disciplines. The technical and

NEW DIRECTIONS FOR HIGHER EDUCATION • DOI 10.1002/he

medical disciplines in general are more open than others, despite being research oriented. The humanities and social sciences believe they know enough about teaching (and are not very attentive to learning), and "classical" science has its own theory about gifted students: that they were born for such disciplines or they have learned the fundamental lessons at school such that the university need not motivate them or teach them to learn. They believe that existing teaching methods are sufficient, since the faculty members themselves studied under such circumstances successfully.

Intensified Links Between Research and Teaching

In Germany there is a long tradition of unity between research and teaching, that is, developing teaching directly out of research or close to research. It means the participation of students directly in research projects. These close connections were the basis of a major reform in higher education in the beginning of the nineteenth century, introduced by Wilhelm von Humboldt, then chief of cultural affairs in the Prussian ministry in Berlin (1808–09). Formerly, teachers in HE in Germany had only teaching duties, with an extremely high number of hours—thirty to thirty-four per week. When von Humboldt came into office, he changed this into a research obligation for every teacher in HE and lowered the teaching load to equal amounts of teaching and research. Hence, the German university of the second half of the nineteenth century was most successful in preparing people for research and industrial application. Alumni were up to date with the most recent research and were useful in all areas of society, particularly when applying their knowledge within an industry. This model of close links between research and teaching was influential for the American university system (Hermann, 2005; Webler, 1986).

Teachers in HE often say that whenever they teach in a lecture or seminar, they learn a lot for their own research in response to students' questions. In many cases, students have an unusual perspective on well-known results, procedures, and cases, which leads to new perspectives. Suddenly new aspects are discovered, which can be fruitful for the teacher.

For about thirty years, two learning concepts with close links between research and teaching have existed in Germany: "generic learning" (students learn about how the original research was done) and "learning by research" (students do research by themselves as part of their studies) (Bundesassistentenkonferenz, 1970). Some study programs exist during which so-called empirical learning research projects (*Lehrforschungsprojekte*) of two or three semesters of six hours per week are obligatory. In these research projects, students prove their abilities as researchers, which means formulating the main research questions, developing questionnaires or other instruments for data collection, collecting the data, analyzing and interpreting the data, and finally presenting the results in a report. The teacher is only a background person who can be asked for guidance in difficult stages of the project. In inquiries at the end of the degree program, when asked when they learned the most about their discipline, students often reply it was during the empirical learning research project. Over the last few years, the problem-based learning (PBL) approach, founded originally on ideas of German and American educators such as Kerschensteiner and Dewey (before and after World War I), has become popular, especially in medical education, such as in the way the medical department of the University at Hamilton, Ontario, has developed it. The way PBL initiates student learning is close to a research-oriented approach (Webler, 2005b).

Possible Tensions Between Research and Teaching Requirements

The traditional combination of research and teaching in German universities remains important because this combination not only motivates teachers but also is an important means of providing students with the most up-to-date knowledge. They may then transfer this knowledge into their professional practice after leaving the university. Research and teaching should therefore remain closely associated. It is worth noting that tensions between the two requirements are possible: curiosity and doubt form an elementary basis for both.

References

Bundesassistentenkonferenz (hrsg.). "Forschendes Lernen: Wissenschaftliches Prüfen." Selbstverlag: Bonn, 1970.

Hermann, U. "Die Einheit von Forschung und Lehre—universitäres Gründungsmotiv und Qualitätsgarantie." Das Hochschulwesen (HSW), 2005, 53(1), 2–8.

Webler, W.-D. "Statik und Dynamik der Hochschulentwicklung: Historisch-soziologische Ursachen für Stabilität und Wandel deutscher Hochschulen." Zeitschrift für Sozialisationsforschung und Erziehungssoziologie (ZSE), 1986, 6(2), 213–238.

Webler, W.-D. "Welches Niveau darf von einem Bachelor-Studium erwartet werden? Wenn Curricula professionell entwickelt, Lehre professionell angeboten und Studium vernünftig angeleitet wäre, dann. . . ." In F. Gützkow and G. Quaißer (hrsg.), Hochschule gestalten. Denkanstösse aus Hochschulpolitik und Hochschulforschung. Bielefeld: UVW Verlag, 2004.

Webler, W.-D. "Chancen von Bachelor- und Masterstudiengängen." In U. von Holdt, C. Stange, and K. Schobel (hrsg.), Qualitative Aspekte von Leistungspunkten: Chancen von Bachelor- und Masterstudiengängen. Bielefeld: UVW Verlag, 2005a.

Webler, W.-D. "Das Erstsemesterprojekt an der Fakultät für Forst- und Umweltwissenschaften der Universität Freiburg. Ein Modell zum selbstgesteuerten Lernen in Projekten." In U. Welbers and O. Gaus (hrsg.), The Shift from Teaching to Learning. Konstruktionsbedingungen eines Ideals. Bielefeld: Wilhelm Bertelsmann, 2005b.

WOLFF-DIETRICH WEBLER is professor of higher education and director of the Bielefeld Institute for Research on Science and Education, Northrhine-Westfalia, Germany.

7

In Finland, quality enhancement is an area of great institutional autonomy.

Enhancing the Quality of Teaching in Higher Education in Finland: The Case of the University of Helsinki

Sari Lindblom-Ylänne

The Finnish National Higher Education Policy aims at raising the general standard of education and promoting educational equality. Efforts have been made to provide all population groups and regions of the country with equal educational opportunities. Each year, 65 percent of the age cohort begin studies at a higher education institution, one-third at the university level and 35 percent at the polytechnic level (Ministry of Education, 2000, 2003).

In many international evaluations, Finland has been found to be the most competitive nation both in business life and in education. For instance, the excellent results obtained by Finnish school children in the international PISA program (Organisation for Economic Co-operation and Development Programme for International Student Assessment) have drawn much attention to the quality of Finnish education. Of the OECD countries, Finland invests the second most in research and development projects in proportion to the gross national product ("Education at a Glance," 2003).

Higher education in Finland is provided by universities and polytechnics. Finland has one of the most comprehensive university networks in Europe, consisting of twenty universities and thirty polytechnics. The total university enrollment is currently approximately 170,000 students. The basic mission of the universities is to carry out research and offer education

NEW DIRECTIONS FOR HIGHER EDUCATION, no. 133, Spring 2006 © Wiley Periodicals, Inc.
Published online in Wiley InterScience (www.interscience.wiley.com) • DOI: 10.1002/he.206

based on that research. The underlying principle in university education is freedom of research and university autonomy, which gives the universities extensive latitude for independent decisions. The Finnish polytechnic system was founded on the institutions that previously furnished postsecondary vocational education and that were developed to form a nationwide network of regional institutions of higher education. Approximately 125,000 students are registered at the thirty polytechnics in Finland (Ministry of Education, 2000).

Tertiary Education Is Free of Charge

Students from diverse socioeconomic backgrounds are able to enter university because tertiary education is free in Finland. Gender equality is also fulfilled; more than half of the students at the tertiary level are female. Studying at a university is highly valued, which may be seen for example in the high number of applicants. The students are selected through demanding entrance examinations. The annual number of applications is nearly sixty-eight thousand, and only twenty-eight thousand candidates are admitted each year.

All Finnish universities are state-run. Public education accounts for 13 percent of all public expenditure. About two-thirds of this consists of state funding and one-third municipal funding. Each university and the Ministry of Education sign a performance agreement in which both parties commit themselves to certain objectives, projects, and level of funding. The agreement is signed for a three-year period, but the financial aspects of the agreement are checked and negotiated every year (Ministry of Education, 2000) with the help of a performance-monitoring database and self-evaluation carried out by the universities. With management determined by results and target setting, the ministry seeks to promote the central aims set for development of education and research in higher education (Ministry of Education, 2004).

The universities are steered by the Universities Act (556/2005), which determines the distribution of educational responsibilities between universities. Correspondingly, the Polytechnics Act and Decree (351/2003) defines the status of the polytechnics in the educational system as well as their teaching, degrees, and evaluation. In addition, field-specific decrees lay down the responsibility for education in a given discipline; degree titles; and the structure, extent, objectives, and content of education.

New Degree Structures on the Basis of the Bologna Declaration

The Bologna Declaration has had a profound impact on degree structures in Finland. Previously, only a few students aimed for a bachelor's degree, and most Finnish graduates have a master's degree. In spring 2003, the

Ministry of Education drew up contracts with all Finnish universities regarding redesign of degrees according to the Bologna Declaration. By autumn 2005, all universities in Finland had adopted a system based on two main cycles, the undergraduate and graduate levels. Access to the second cycle requires successful completion of first-cycle studies. The bachelor-level studies are to last three years, while the second two-year cycle leads to the master's degree. In other words, the bachelor's degree is viewed as an intermediate stage on the way to the master's degree, which in Finland will still be the main university degree. After the master's degree, it is possible to apply for four-year doctoral studies.

The Ministry of Education lent additional financial support to universities for 2004 and 2005 for designing the new degrees. With the help of this financial support, the University of Helsinki, for instance, was able to recruit approximately twenty academic staff members from several disciplines who were hired by the faculties to coordinate and support design of the new degrees.

In addition, the Ministry of Education gave financial support for national coordination of degree development in the disciplines. The University of Helsinki is coordinating the most extensive reform process, that of education and teacher training. Three full-time academic staff members have been recruited for three years to enhance national coordination of the reform process (Lindblom-Ylänne and Hämäläinen, 2004).

Quality Assurance in Higher Education in Finland

The national quality assurance system of higher education consists of the national higher education policy, national evaluations, and quality assurance implemented at the level of individual institutions of higher education. The ministry takes care of quantitative evaluation of higher education institutions. As a part of a renewed national quality assurance system, the Ministry of Education will develop methods and criteria for decisions on starting new programs, ending old ones, and evaluating existing programs in special cases.

The Finnish Higher Education Evaluation Council (FINHEEC) is responsible for evaluating the quality of education and other activities in higher education institutions. FINHEEC organizes audits of quality work and institutional, program, and thematic evaluations. In addition, it supports higher education institutions in designing their quality assurance systems, offers training seminars on evaluation, and maintains a library and information service. FINHEEC aims at developing evaluation methodology and disseminating good practices. To achieve this, it offers financial support to development projects implemented by higher education institutions. FINHEEC allocates funding for development projects on the basis of current themes, such as development of quality assurance systems. Every year three to five projects are given financial support of approximately €30,000 each. The final reports of these projects are distributed in the FINHEEC publication series to disseminate good practices (http://www.kka.fi/english/index.lasso?cont=index).

Furthermore, FINHEEC selects a maximum of twenty national high-quality units in university and polytechnic education every third year. Each high-quality unit receives extra yearly funding of approximately €85,000– 500,000 varying according to the size of the university. The total yearly amount of funding for the high-quality units is €6 million. The units may use the extra funding any way they want for development of teaching and learning at the institutes—for example, to hire new teachers to decrease the workload of academic staff (http://www.kka.fi/english/index.lasso?cont=index).

Institutions of higher education bear the main responsibility for the quality of their activities. Universities are currently developing quality assurance systems, which will cover all institutional activities: education, research, and societal services.

In contrast to universities, all the polytechnics were accredited by FINHEEC when the polytechnic sector was established in the late 1990s. In addition to these institutional evaluations, every higher education institution has participated in the several other types of evaluation. According to legislation, higher education institutions are required to take part in the national evaluations. FINHEEC has started to audit the quality assurance systems of universities and polytechnics. All systems will be audited by the year 2010; follow-up evaluations will take place every three years.

Enhancement of the Quality of Teaching and Learning at the University of Helsinki

The University of Helsinki is the oldest and largest university in Finland. It was founded in 1640 and has thirty-eight thousand students and approximately seventy-five hundred staff members spread across four campuses. The university concentrates on high-level scientific research and researcher education and is a member of the League of European Research Universities (LERU), a cooperative body of leading European research universities (http://www.leru.org/). The university renews its program for development of teaching and studies every three years. The program is launched by the university senate. According to the ambitious objectives of the current program ("Programme for Development . . . ," 2003), the University of Helsinki aims to create a stimulating atmosphere for teaching and learning. The emphasis is on turning away from a teacher-centered approach toward a more student-centered approach to teaching. It is further emphasized that teaching should be research-based and that management of teaching and quality assurance should be developed. By research-based teaching, the university refers first to the principle that every one of the academic staff does research and teaches, second to emphasis on linking teaching with the latest research, and third to the aim that students should be given ample opportunity to practice and develop their research skills and participate in the work of the research groups in their departments. The aim is further to enhance teachers' teaching skills and their ability to use information and communication technologies (ICTs) ("Programme for Development . . . ," 2003).

The program also requires future action resulting from a recent international evaluation of teaching and degrees in the faculties (Tuomi and Pakkanen, 2002). The university has a tradition of carrying out international evaluations on the quality of its research, teaching, and administration every six years. For example, for evaluation of teaching and degrees the university was divided into fifteen disciplinary areas. Thus fifteen evaluation panels, consisting of seventy-seven members representing expertise in the fields under evaluation and in university-level instruction, were assembled (Tuomi and Pakkanen, 2002). The university requires that the faculties construct their three-year development projects on the basis of evaluation results. In this way it is possible to make sure that the developmental challenges noticed by the evaluation panels are taken seriously and incorporated in developing learning and instruction in the faculties.

The results of the international evaluation of the quality of research affect funding of faculties, whereas the results of the evaluations of the quality of teaching do not directly affect it, even though recent discussions have considered changing the current practice. However, the results of the evaluations of the quality of teaching have an indirect effect on funding of the faculties in that the funding granted for each faculty is dependent on the yearly number of degrees conferred. If the quality of teaching is not high, this has an effect on the learning outcomes of students. If students do not receive enough high-quality teaching, counseling, and support in their learning processes, their study pace may slow down and they will not graduate in the expected study time. In addition, some students may even drop out.

In addition, the rector of the university grants extra funding of €150,000 to be divided between four to eight high-quality teaching departments or units of the university on the basis of the self-evaluations carried out by these units. The criteria applied in selecting these units are from the teaching evaluation matrix, which is the core of the quality assurance system of the university. The matrix defines high-quality teaching as, for example, being closely linked with the latest research, being student-centered, and providing ample feedback and support for students (http://www.helsinki.fi/arviointi/koulutuksen_laadunvarmistus/arviointimatriisi.htm). The university also gives yearly prizes (in total €21,000) for projects that enhance and develop use of ICT in teaching and learning.

To support educational development and research in the faculties, the University of Helsinki has invested significantly in the development of teaching and learning and in research in teaching and learning. The university has a Centre for Research and Development of Higher Education. The center fosters research on learning and instruction in higher education and improves university teachers' skills and their understanding of the various factors related to successful studying and high-quality teaching. It carries out research on teaching and learning in higher education and coordinates the pedagogical training of academic staff. All pedagogical training programs of the academic staff are approved by the center.

Furthermore, it plays a strategic role in the institutionwide changes that are taking place (Lindblom-Ylänne and Hämäläinen, 2004). Discipline-specific development units are situated on the campuses, employing a total of about thirty staff. Of these, some (particularly at the medical campus) work half-time in the campus units and half-time in their own department. On the largest central campus, which comprises five faculties, the faculties also have their own development units. The Centre for Research and Development of Higher Education coordinates and supports discipline-specific development efforts and research, and there is a strong disciplinary focus in all such work. Furthermore, the center carries out research on learning and instruction in higher education together with staff from the campus development units. For example, an ongoing research project aims at examining discipline-based approaches to teaching in research-intensive universities, the effects of pedagogical training, teaching experience, and the characteristics of the learning environment in teachers' approaches to teaching (see, for example, Elen, Lindblom-Ylänne, and Clement, 2005; Lindblom-Ylänne, Trigwell, Nevgi, and Ashwin, in press; Postareff, Lindblom-Ylänne, and Nevgi, in press). To summarize, the approach of the university is a balance of decentralized and centralized support for academic development (Hicks, 1999).

The university gives its staff various kinds of workshops, seminars, and courses related to enhancement of teaching and learning in higher education and to university pedagogy. In addition to short seminars, teachers as well as doctoral students may participate in courses on university pedagogy organized by the Centre for Research and Development of Higher Education and by campus development units. The basic teacher-training course, which lasts six months and carries ten ECTS (European Credit Transfer System) credits, focuses on theoretical principles of learning and instruction and gives teachers the basic skills to plan, instruct, and assess teaching and learning in their courses. Teachers may continue their studies on university pedagogy by participating in two advanced courses, which are offered only by the Centre for Research and Development of Higher Education. The second course (fifteen ECTS credits) takes one year and aims at deepening teachers' understanding of theoretical principles of learning and instruction in higher education. Finally, teachers who want to achieve scholarship in university teaching can complete a two-year course (thirty-five ECTS credits). The content of this course is tailored for each participant to take into account discipline-based approaches to teaching and the individual interests of the teacher as well as his or her level of pedagogical knowledge and skills (Lindblom-Ylänne and Hämäläinen, 2004).

Participation in pedagogical training is not mandatory for teachers. However, the university encourages faculties to take teaching skill and merit into consideration when filling academic posts. In 1999, the University of Helsinki Senate made a series of decisions concerning development of teaching and research posts and related procedures at the university. According to these decisions, assessment of academic competence for the purpose of analyzing wage developments must be based on academic portfolios. This entails lecturers and professors compiling an academic portfolio of their qualifications and keeping it up to date.

The same year, to enhance the quality of teaching and learning in numerous disciplines, the university created a pool of teaching posts consisting of fifteen fixed-term senior lecturers (which equates to the position of associate professor) who have broad experience in educational development in higher education. The total number of fifteen senior lectureships is kept constant, but these posts are set for a period of five years so that three new allocations of posts are made every year. Faculties and independent institutes may make proposals for allocation and use of the available lecturers' posts in connection with their annual finance and policy plans, which include development plans for teaching and studies as well as related project proposals. The disciplinary background of these senior lecturers varies mainly from education and psychology to social psychology, but they may also represent other disciplines, such as pharmacy and veterinary medicine. Whatever the disciplinary background, these lecturers have gained expertise in educational development in higher education.

The university senate decides on allocation of posts from the pool. The most important criterion is that the proposal must be based on the Programme for the Development of Teaching and Studies of the university to ensure alignment with educational development projects (Lindblom-Ylänne and Hämäläinen, 2004).

Once allocated, these senior lecturers become key persons in developing teaching and learning in the disciplines and in carrying out research on educational development in their faculties. The scope of their duties may be so broad as to cover systematic development of teaching at the faculty level or within a discipline, or it may be narrowed down to development of a clearly defined area, such as assessment practices, supervision practices, postgraduate education, or application of ICT in higher education. Of key importance is that the senior lecturers cooperate actively with teachers and students in the faculties, aiming at enhancing and developing discipline-specific approaches to learning and instruction (Lindblom-Ylänne and Hämäläinen, 2004).

Because the senior lecturers are situated in the faculties, it is important to ensure their integration with other personnel involved in educational development at the university. The Centre for Research and Development in Higher Education coordinates and enhances cooperation between these staff members. Together, they all form a network of experts in university-level teaching that makes its know-how available to the entire academic community. Their expertise is a valuable asset to the university when faculties and departments require consultation in university teaching methods, professional supervision, or training.

Future Challenges in Educational Development in Finland

The University of Helsinki is a pioneer in offering its academic staff opportunities to participate in courses on university pedagogy and, in this way, developing scholarship in university teaching. There is not yet a national pedagogical training program for university teachers, but Finnish universities have started to cooperate to build one in the future. A nationwide association entitled Peda-Forum is a network of university staff interested in educational development. This association publishes a journal twice a year for university staff and organizes yearly conferences on teaching matters where it is possible to share research results and experiences in developing teaching and learning in higher education.

A major challenge in Finland is to start systematically taking teaching merit into account in filling academic posts. In this way, it is possible to motivate a larger number of university teachers to develop their teaching skills and enhance their understanding of teaching and learning in higher education.

References

"Education at a Glance." Paris: Organisation for Economic Co-operation and Development, 2003.

Elen, J., Lindblom-Ylänne, S., and Clement, M. (2005). "Research-Intensive Teaching: An Exploration in Two Research-Intensive Universities." Manuscript submitted for publication, 2005.

Hicks, O. "Integration of Central and Departmental Development: Reflections from Australian Universities." *International Journal for Academic Development*, 1999, 4(1), 43–51.

Lindblom-Ylänne, S., and Hämäläinen, K. "The Bologna Declaration as a Tool to Enhance Learning and Instruction at the University of Helsinki." *International Journal for Academic Development*, 2004, 9(2), 151–164.

Lindblom-Ylänne, S., Trigwell, K., Nevgi, A., and Ashwin, P. "How Approaches to Teaching are Affected by Discipline and Teaching Context." *Studies in Higher Education*, in press.

Ministry of Education. "Higher Education Policy in Finland." Helsinki: Nykypaino, 2000. http://www.minedu.fi/julkaisut/Hep2001/Pdf/HEP.pdf.

Ministry of Education. "Ministry of Education Strategy 2015." Finland 2003:35. Helsinki: Helsinki University Press, 2003. http://www.minedu.fi/julkaisut/hallinto/2003/opm35/opm35.pdf.

Ministry of Education. "Management and Steering of Higher Education in Finland." 2004:20. Helsinki: Helsinki University Printing House, 2004. http://www.minedu.fi/julkaisut/koulutus/2004/opm20/opm20.pdf.

Postareff, L., Lindblom-Ylänne, S., and Nevgi, A. "The Effect of Pedagogical Training on Teaching in Higher Education." *Teaching and Teacher Education,* in press.

"Programme for Development of Teaching and Studies at the University of Helsinki 2004–2006." Helsinki: Helsinki University Printing House, 2003.

Tuomi, O., and Pakkanen, P. *Towards Excellence in Teaching: Evaluation of the Quality of Education and the Degree Programmes in the University of Helsinki.* Publications of Finnish Higher Education Evaluation Council (FINHEEC) no. 18. Helsinki: Helsinki University Printing House, 2002. http:www.kka.fi.

SARI LINDBLOM-YLÄNNE is professor and director of the Centre for Research and Development of Higher Education, Department of Education, Faculty of Behavioural Sciences, at the University of Helsinki, Finland.

8

*For Flanders, the Bologna declaration has launched an
innovation process carrying unprecedented challenges for
higher education.*

Stimulating the Quality of University Teaching in Flanders, Belgium

Piet Verhesschen

Belgium is a country with ten million inhabitants. Brussels is not only the capital of the country but also the host for several European institutions. As a result of a number of revisions of the constitution, Belgium is a federal state. The federal state, the communities, and the regions have powers and responsibilities for different policy areas. The communities are demarcated by "language," and so we talk about Flemish, French, and German-speaking communities. Since 1989, education has fallen under the jurisdiction of these communities, which means the Flemish government is independent from the federal state when it comes to education. The Flemish Minister for Education is responsible for every aspect of educational policy, from nursery to higher education. This means that although there is much similarity in the educational system of Belgium as a whole since it used to be uniform (in terms of general structure of the system and length of studies), there are differences between Flanders, the French-speaking community, and the German-speaking community. With respect to the law on higher education, there is similar but still slightly differing legislation in these parts of the country. (There is no university in the small German-speaking community.) The Flemish community lives in Flanders, the northern and largest part of Belgium. This chapter focuses on the situation in Flanders.

In Flanders there are twenty-two so-called *hogescholen* (institutions for nonuniversity higher education) and six universities. Hogescholen offer higher education courses and should not be confused with high schools.

New Directions for Higher Education, no. 133, Spring 2006 © Wiley Periodicals, Inc.
Published online in Wiley InterScience (www.interscience.wiley.com) • DOI: 10.1002/he.207

Some would like to call the hogescholen universities, but the already existing universities are reluctant to share their privilege. (In the Netherlands, where similar hogescholen exist, they are allowed to promote themselves as universities of professional education.) In 2004 the hogescholen had 103,550 students in basic programs, and the universities had approximately 57,600 students in the basic programs. Ghent University (with approximately 20,200 students in basic programs) and the Katholieke Universiteit Leuven (with about 21,600 students in basic programs) are the largest universities in Flanders (Ministerie van de Vlaamse Gemeenschap, 2005). The participation rate in higher education is approximately 67 percent. In all Belgian universities, student entry is open, rather than competitive. As a consequence of this open entry, there is considerable dropping out after the first year. At the K. U. Leuven for instance, 56 percent of the students succeed in their first year (ranging from 48 percent to 87 percent, depending on the field of study). In the second year, however, the success rate is 83 percent (K. U. Leuven, 2004). Another consequence of this open entry is large class size, especially in the first and second years.

The K. U. Leuven is the only Flemish member of the League of European Research Universities (with twelve members). With 38 percent of the Flemish professors, the K. U. Leuven is responsible for 45 percent of the Flemish research output. Therefore, the K. U. Leuven can be considered research-intensive. But the labels of research-intensive and teaching university are rarely used in stressing the distinctive features of the institutions in Flanders. All Flemish universities have three tasks: research, teaching, and service to society. The K. U. Leuven affirms itself as an academic institution where research that opens up new horizons and knowledge transfer are essential and complementary. Teaching is based on and nourished by its own research and by an interdisciplinary approach.

Quality Assurance in Universities

With regard to the policy concerning higher education, the framework within which universities can operate is formed by several laws. Called decrees, they deal with the structure of higher education, the financing of universities, and the rights of students and staff. Within this framework universities have always claimed a considerable degree of autonomy.

Although initiatives in the field of quality assurance date from the 1980s, a systematic and overall approach to quality assurance at Flemish universities was introduced as a government policy only in 1991. Flemish universities obtained more autonomy in exchange for adopting a more systematic approach to quality assurance and enhancement. Universities were explicitly made responsible for developing internal and external quality assurance mechanisms with respect to their teaching activities. Determination of the internal quality mechanism and procedures is left to each university.

For the external quality assurance system, universities have to organize evaluations jointly (external peer review). These evaluations are coordinated by the Flemish Interuniversity Council. External evaluation of a program is carried out by a commission of peers from other universities, with administrative support from the Flemish Interuniversity Council. They visit all universities that offer a similar program and their final report (including a comparison between programs) is made public (Hulpiau and others, 2005). The external evaluation consists of three steps. First, each program undergoes a critical self-analysis. In this analysis, academic and administrative staff, students, graduates, and representatives of the profession are involved. It lasts about a year and the result is a report submitted to the external commission. This report deals with the aims and learning outcomes of the program, the curriculum, deployment of staff, infrastructure, internal quality assurance mechanisms, and program output. In a second step, this external commission visits the program onsite. On the basis of the self-report and the site visit, the commission writes a final report that is made public (the newspapers pay attention to the main findings). Every eight years, each program is evaluated in this way. In the near future, the final evaluation report will be the starting point for an accreditation procedure (this is discussed later). For the external evaluation as well as for the accreditation, Flanders and the Netherlands cooperate.

Although the universities have a high degree of autonomy, quality assurance initiatives are a legal obligation. The idea is that in return for public funding society has the right to expect university teaching of high quality.

Funding of Universities

For the K. U. Leuven 77 percent of total funding comes from the government.

In principle, funding of universities is based on the number of students (however, because a new system of financing of higher education will commence in 2007, the level of funding has remained unchanged for the past few years). Students pay a registration fee of €505 for a full-time program. Students on a grant from the government pay €80. Boundaries for tuition fees are determined by law. To avoid competition between universities on the basis of tuition fees, universities make agreements about this.

At present there is no direct link between external quality assessment and funding, but in the public debate with respect to the financing of universities this is an issue. Because in the near future only programs with accreditation will be allowed to deliver diplomas, and because the evaluation report will be the basis for the accreditation procedure, quality of teaching can have an impact on university funding. If output becomes a parameter in the new system of financing, quality of teaching and learning will have an indirect impact on the funding of universities.

The Bologna Process and Its Implementation in Flanders

In July 1999, the minister of education of Flanders was one of the twenty-nine European ministers who signed the "Bologna Declaration." The main objectives of this declaration are adoption of a system of easily readable and comparable degrees, a system essentially based on two main cycles (under-graduate and graduate), establishment of a system of credits such as in the ECTS system, promotion of mobility for students and staff, promotion of European cooperation in quality assurance with a view to developing com-parable criteria and methodologies, and promotion of European dimensions in higher education. As a result, the Flemish government and Flemish uni-versities began to prepare for higher education reform in accordance with the Bologna objectives. The most visible step was acceptance by the Flemish Parliament of the decree on the structure of higher education, on April 4, 2003. Without dealing with the decree in detail, we can say that there are four major innovations. First, the decree changes the length of the programs by introducing bachelor's (180 ECTS credits) and master's programs (60 or 120 ECTS credits depending on the field of study).

A second major change introduced by the decree is the transition from a threefold structure (higher education courses lasting one cycle in hoge-scholen, higher education courses of two cycles in hogescholen, and uni-versity programs) to a twofold structure (professional higher education programs and academic higher education programs). As a consequence, the former two-cycle programs in nonuniversity higher education are obliged to become more academic. This shift to research-based programs has a major impact on the importance of research, the qualification of the staff (in the future, a Ph.D. becomes a prerequisite), and the curricula. These pro-grams are thus facing a challenge to implement the link between research and teaching. To facilitate this process, working groups of university pro-fessors and their colleagues from the hogescholen are created to increase the research-based character of programs at the latter institutions. Indeed, as determined by law, it is the responsibility of the universities to support this process in the context of an "association."

Creation of associations is therefore the third innovation introduced by the decree. Every university in Flanders has to become a member of an asso-ciation. An association is cooperation between a university and one or more hogescholen. The associations are seen by the government as a way to cre-ate synergy between the institutions of higher education in developing coherent programs. As a result there are five associations in Flanders. Together with twelve hogescholen, the K. U. Leuven forms the K. U. Leuven Association. With 45 percent of students in higher education, the K. U. Leuven Association is the largest in Flanders.

NEW DIRECTIONS FOR HIGHER EDUCATION • DOI 10.1002/he

The reform of the quality assurance system in cooperation with the Netherlands is a fourth important innovation of the decree. We have already mentioned that in the future bachelor's and master's degrees can be granted only by institutions that have obtained an accreditation that guarantees the quality of the program. Each program in higher education, academic as well as professional, will be visited and accredited every eight years (Verhesschen and Verburgh, 2004). In September 2003 a new governmental accreditation body, *Nederlands Vlaams accreditatie orgaan,* was installed.

Stimulation of Educational Innovation

The decree also proposes additional funding for higher education institutions on the condition that they submit to the government an educational development plan (for the period 2003–2006). In this plan the institutions describe how they will transform existing programs into the new bachelor's-master's structure and what initiatives they will take with regard to educational innovation and greater flexibility of the programs. Innovation is understood as curriculum development with respect to content, learning approaches, forms of student evaluation and assessment, support for students, and so on. Greater flexibility aims at developing ways to reach new target groups and suitable course materials or e-learning. In this way the ministry of education uses the incentive of additional funding as an instrument to motivate institutions of higher education to invest in innovation. Similarly, institutions are invited to develop long-term plans for quality assurance.

Professional Development at the Institutional Level

In 1997, long before the government initiative for additional funding, the K. U. Leuven introduced the possibility for academic staff to obtain funding for innovative educational projects. At the start, the projects were funded by the university. Since the government initiative of extra funding, the university has decided to use part of these resources for this purpose. Other universities have since introduced similar initiatives.

In my own university, as the result of an initiative of the Educational Council, the concept of "guided independent learning" was accepted in 1999 by the Academic Board (being the highest academic authority in the university) as the overarching educational concept for the entire university. Confronted with growing concern over the quality of university teaching, the educational concept was the result of an attempt to make the view of the K. U. Leuven on good university education explicit.

As the result of reflection on the role of the university in a changing scientific and societal context and taking into account recent developments in instructional psychology, the concept describes the aims of university education and the respective roles of students and professors. In a nutshell, this concept recognizes that in the end the individual student is responsible for his or her own learning process, but that it is the responsibility of the staff to provide optimal support for the student to actively engage in the learning process (Elen, 2003). The concept of guided independent learning also stresses the importance of the relation between research and education. This concept is the frame of reference for all decisions with respect to teaching. All curricular decisions across programs, for instance, need to take this into account.

Since the acceptance of this educational concept, the university has undertaken several initiatives to facilitate implementation. Competitive distribution of extra funding for innovative educational projects is one way to further application of the concept. Since the introduction, there have been eight rounds of such projects. As in the previous rounds, a sum of €1,500,000 is made available for the ninth round. Last year, fourteen projects out of forty-seven applications were selected. The duration of the project depends on its aims, but the maximum is two years.

The educational innovation projects thus are part of an elaborated educational policy plan. In this way, academic staff are encouraged to experiment with new approaches in teaching. In addition, the Educational Support Office of the K. U. Leuven has developed a range of initiatives for professional development of academic staff. The office is a central unit, independent of any department, with some twenty staff members. They offer support in the field of educational innovation, curriculum development, quality assurance, and professional development. The unit offers workshops and seminars. At present these initiatives are not compulsory for professors, but it could become a policy issue.

This illustrates that opportunities for academic staff to engage in inquiry on teaching and learning or professional development projects are not available on the state level, although government funds can be used for this purpose. Nevertheless it is up to the institutions themselves to decide whether or not to offer these opportunities. Notwithstanding the practice of cooperation between universities in the domain of research, collaboration aimed at enhancing teaching and learning does not exist. Since the creation of the K. U. Leuven Association, collaboration has been established among member institutions with respect to professional development, quality assurance, tuning of programs, and so on. The association has also created a fund for financing educational innovation projects. But again, this is an element of the educational policy of the association.

The availability of resources necessary to start several initiatives aimed at implementing the university's educational concept of guided independent learning has proven to be an important instrument for educational policy at the university. At the K. U. Leuven, eight years of funding of educational innovation projects has resulted in some eighty projects. A number of them

NEW DIRECTIONS FOR HIGHER EDUCATION • DOI 10.1002/he

have led to valuable results, for instance in the use of ICT, case-based learning, collaborative learning, student-centered learning, and so on. A major concern is their continuity. Such funding offers the opportunity to develop innovative learning environments, which often leads to valuable results. But integration of these new practices into regular teaching as well as dissemination of good practice once the initial project phase is over is not guaranteed. We are currently investigating continuation of these project results.

Challenges

In a context of accountability, professors are under heavy pressure. They are confronted with high expectations for research and teaching. Research output of professors and research centers is increasingly based on bibliometric data. Despite this context of publish-or-perish, teaching staff who are concerned about the quality of their teaching are prepared to invest in preparation of their courses and in professional development in order to improve their teaching skills. But a necessary precondition is transparency about the extent to and the way in which teaching is acknowledged. The most important element in recruiting new academic staff is their research achievements and their list of publications. Also in decisions with respect to promotion and tenure, the research output is the first criterion. Professors are willing to invest in their teaching on the condition that their efforts be appreciated and taken into account (Hulpiau and others, 2005).

As mentioned earlier, the transition from a threefold structure to a twofold structure in higher education will probably have consequences for the relationships among programs and institutions. Since, for instance, not only universities but also nonuniversity institutions of higher education are allowed to offer academic programs, it remains to be seen whether this will have an effect on enrollment.

The fact that nonuniversity institutions also offer academic programs has revived reflection on the peculiarities of academic teaching and learning compared to professional education. Renewed interest in research-based teaching and in the link between research and teaching and learning is an aspect of this. The Bologna process brings along a discourse with terms such as "employability" of graduates, "competency based learning," and "learning outcomes." According to some, this shift to utilitarianism puts the concept of academic or university education under pressure. They fear that recent developments in higher education will lead to a vocational drift in academic programs.

Another result of the Bologna process is growing awareness of the European and global context of the university. The Bologna process will lead to greater comparability and convergence of programs in higher education in the forty-five participating countries. In the near future, programs aiming at foreign students will become more important, and this will have an impact on the curricula and language used in higher education institutions. It can also be expected that the discourse on the knowledge economy and on the necessity of lifelong learning will lead to new kinds of students. Programs and organization of studies will have to be adapted to their characteristics. In this context, the current trend toward acknowledgment of prior learning should be mentioned.

Institutions for higher education will also have to take into account the growing mobility of their own students.

We have already mentioned the importance of accreditation as a precondition for the right to deliver diplomas or grant degrees. This means that ultimately the quality of a program can have consequences for the mere survival of the program or an institution. Accountability thus becomes more important, and this puts initiatives aimed at quality improvement or enhancement under pressure. Institutions for higher education have a moral obligation to offer their students the best possible education; hence programs must meet the standards. External visitation stimulates regular revision of the program and can prevent the quality of the program being taken for granted. But the emphasis on accountability can invade and diminish the space for honest and critical self-evaluation. Since accreditation is the goal, acknowledgment of weaknesses as the starting point for a process of improvement can be replaced by affirmation of strengths. If academic staff can no longer experiment with new teaching approaches without fear, the stress on accountability will hinder educational innovation.

References

Elen, J. "Reality of Excellence in Higher Education: The Case of Guided Independent Learning at the Katholieke Universiteit Leuven." In E. De Corte (ed.), *Excellence in Higher Education: Proceedings from a Symposium held at the Wenner-Gren Centre, Stockholm, 2002*. London: Portland, 2003.

Hulpiau, V., and others. "A System of Student Feedback: Considerations of Academic Staff Taken into Account." Paper presented at EAIR forum, Riga, Latvia, Aug. 29, 2005.

K. U. Leuven. *Jaarrapport 2004*. (Annual Report 2004.) Leuven: K. U. Leuven, 2004.

Ministerie van de Vlaamse Gemeenschap departement Onderwijs. *Beperkte statistische telling hoger onderwijs—academiejaar 2004–2005*. [Limited Statistical Counting Higher Education—Year 2004–05]. Brussels: Ministerie van de Vlaamse Gemeenschap, 2005.

Verhesschen, P., and Verburgh, A. "The Introduction of the Bachelor-Master's Structure at the K. U. Leuven: Challenges and Opportunities for Faculty Development." *International Journal for Academic Development*, 2004, 9(2), 131–149.

Piet Verhesschen is director of the Office for Educational Policy at the Katholieke Universiteit Leuven, Belgium. He is involved in introducing the bachelor-master structure at his university.

9

A new philosophical perspective is suggested that would transform and Africanize curricula, teaching, and learning in South African universities.

University Teaching in South Africa: An African Philosophical Perspective

Philip Higgs, Berte van Wyk

Recent developments indicate that there are historical, institutional, and cultural differences that influence teaching and learning in South African universities. There are also differing beliefs about how relevance and responsiveness are constituted, and about the pedagogical principles that should apply in transferring knowledge (Council on Higher Education, 2004). In recognition of these differences, we argue in this chapter that an African perspective can make a significant contribution to teaching and learning in South African universities.

Background

Higher education in South Africa came under renewed scrutiny during the transition from apartheid to democracy. Many institutions took an active stance against apartheid and were clearly aligned with the democratization of South African society. There was therefore a belief that "the overall well-being of nations is vitally dependent on the contribution of higher education to the social, political, and economic development of its citizens" and "the vital importance of higher education to democracy, social justice, and the economic and social development of this country" (CHE, 2000, p. 2).

The process of transformation of higher education is a feature of the broader project of social transformation. This chapter, in arguing for an

NEW DIRECTIONS FOR HIGHER EDUCATION, no. 133, Spring 2006 © Wiley Periodicals, Inc.
Published online in Wiley InterScience (www.interscience.wiley.com) • DOI: 10.1002/he.208

African perspective on teaching, explores the policy context, institutional landscape, funding, and quality—all features that influence teaching in the new South Africa.

The Policy Context

The formal process of higher education policy began when the promised National Commission on Higher Education (NCHE) was established by presidential proclamation at the end of 1994. Its report, "A Framework for Transformation," submitted in September 1996, rests on three envisaged "pillars" for a transformed higher education system. First, to satisfy the needs of equity, redress, and development, a policy of increased participation was required. This should be achieved through changing from an elite to a mass higher education system, that is, a process of "massification." Second, the NCHE believed that a policy of greater responsiveness was needed to ensure that higher education engaged with the challenges of its social context. This would require changes in the context, focus, and delivery modes of academic programs and research, adapted to the knowledge needs of the market and civil society. The NCHE's third pillar, increased cooperation and partnerships, led to recommendation of a model of "cooperative governance," whose elements included the state in a supervisory role (as opposed to a role of control, or interference), intermediary bodies between state and higher education institutions (HEIs), HEIs characterized by internal constituency partnerships, and a set of linkages between HEIs and civil society.

The Department of Education's "Education White Paper 3" of 1997 set out policy in support of an intention to transform higher education through development of a program-based higher education system, planned, funded, and governed as a single coordinated system. As a necessary means to overcome the deficiencies of the apartheid legacy, the white paper affirmed the principles that must underpin change initiatives: equity and redress, democratization, effectiveness and efficiency, development, quality, academic freedom, institutional autonomy, and public accountability.

After the white paper there was a four-year gap before publication of the next key policy framework, the National Plan for Higher Education (Ministry of Education, 2001). This "implementation vacuum" led to a number of developments. First, there was an absence of regulatory instruments. Second, some HEIs seized market opportunities. Third, rapid shifts in student enrollment occurred, with the number of African and women students in historically advantaged institutions (HAIs) rising significantly, while enrollment at most historically black universities (HBUs) declined sharply. This decline was in part due to financial constraints students faced, but also because students now had greater choice of institution. Other factors included improved access to higher education from the early 1990s, student and parental perceptions of declining quality at HBUs, increased competition from private providers, and expansion of the National Student Financial Aid Scheme (NSFAS).

The period after the national plan can be regarded as focusing on implementation of the transformation agenda, which rests on the three pillars discussed earlier, and the vision that a transformed, democratic, nonracial, and nonsexist system of higher education will (1) promote equity; (2) meet national development needs through well-planned and coordinated teaching, learning, and research programs; (3) support a democratic ethos and a culture of human rights; and (4) contribute to advancement of all forms of knowledge and scholarship.

Institutional Landscape

Prior to 1994, higher education institutions could be classified as historically white (advantaged) or historically black (disadvantaged) universities and "technikons" (universities of technology). The historically white institutions could be subdivided according to medium of instruction into Afrikaans or English institutions, while the historically black institutions could be subdivided according to race: those for Africans (for example, Medunsa; the universities of the North, Vista, and Zululand; Fort Hare, Transkei, Ciskei, and Venda), for "Coloreds" (University of the Western Cape), and for Indians (University of Durban-Westville).

By 1994, the South African higher education landscape consisted of thirty-six public HEIs. They were structured along racial and ethnic lines and were characterized by a rigid binary divide between universities and technikons (fifteen); they were administered by the relevant national authority (eight government departments, in the Republic of South Africa or one of the apartheid "bantustans"; CHE, 2004).

By 2004 the higher education landscape changed considerably and now consists of twenty-two public institutions: eleven universities, five technikons, six comprehensive institutions (combining both university and technikon programs, and in some cases resulting from a university-technikon merger), and two national institutes (in Mpumalanga and the Northern Cape).

A critical challenge is to see how this new institutional landscape addresses challenges with respect to equity, redress, effectiveness, and efficiency.

Funding

Public HEIs receive government funding. Two broad types of government funding were in place up to 1994. First, there were negotiated budgets associated with historically black universities and technikons. Second, there was a funding formula associated initially with the historically white universities: the South African Postsecondary Education (SAPSE) funding formula.

A new goal-oriented, performance-related funding framework is being implemented from 2004, and current debate about financing higher education is dominated by consideration of the nature and effectiveness of this framework. The new funding framework retains the two main components of the SAPSE framework: block grants, and funding earmarked for specific purposes. However, it differs from the SAPSE model in its policy underpinnings, with the consequence that these components are to be applied differently. On average, government grants cover about 50 percent of public higher education funding, with 25 percent from fee income and 25 percent from other private sources (CHE, 2004).

Students are required to pay their own tuition fees. In the late 1980s and early 1990s, several universities incurred increasing debt to nonpayment by students and were forced to restructure by offering voluntary severance packages as well as not filling vacant positions. To assist students, the National Student Financial Aid Scheme (NSFAS) was constituted in 2000, but this has proved to be inadequate.

As elsewhere in the world, government funding decreased after 2000; this has obvious implications for student access. Periodically this leads to student protests and calls on the government to increase funding to enable students to pay for their education.

Quality of Teaching and Learning

We agree with the CHE (2004) that a serious higher education transformation agenda must prioritize quality as a key policy driver. Until 1994 universities guaranteed their own quality standards. This situation was obviously not satisfactory, and it resulted in an ad hoc way of assessing quality. In addition (CHE, 2004) all HEIs had relationships (formal and informal) with professional boards and associations in such areas as medicine, nursing, accounting, and engineering. In 2001, the Higher Education Quality Committee (HEQC) was established, with its mandated roles being (1) accreditation (of programs), (2) audit (of institutions), and (3) quality promotion and capacity development. The HEQC mandate covers the entire spectrum of higher education institutions.

The HEQC definition of quality rests on four objectives: fitness of purpose, fitness for purpose, value for money, and transformation. There is an important distinction between the first two. Fitness *of* purpose refers to quality within the context of national goals for the higher education system, including equity, access, effectiveness, and efficiency (responsiveness). Fitness *for* purpose refers to quality in relation to a specified institutional mission within a national framework that encompasses differentiation and diversity.

NEW DIRECTIONS FOR HIGHER EDUCATION • DOI 10.1002/he

Earlier policies accentuated the equity objective, which has to be aligned with quality. The CHE (2004) argues that equity without quality is meaningless and quality cannot be pursued in isolation from the goal of equity in higher education. A second challenge is to develop, in a differentiated way, a variety of standards appropriate to specified educational objectives and changes.

In 2005 quality assurance exercises were conducted by the HEQC: a national review of master's of education (M.Ed.) programs at all HEIs, audits of some institutions (such as Stellenbosch University), and departmental evaluations at some institutions (Stellenbosch, Cape Town, Wits). These exercises took on the format of self-evaluation and site visits by external reviewers. The HEQC works on a six-year cycle; the M.Ed. program reviews in 2005 will be followed by the bachelor's of education (B.Ed.) reviews in 2006. The outcome of the M.Ed. reviews may be that some universities may not receive accreditation to continue with their programs. This is on the rationale that students deserve quality education, and programs not conforming to acceptable standards do not serve this objective.

University Teaching and African Philosophy

Diversification of the student profile in higher education presents an enormous challenge to teaching. We agree with Barnett (1992) that teaching can be construed as the complex of processes and abilities that bring about higher-order learning. According to Laurillard (2000), the learning process at university level is not a unidirectional transfer of information but an active engagement of the student in the operational aspects of the subject matter, and in the articulation of its theoretical aspects. The two together yield a reflective, adaptive understanding that enhances practice. The question arises: How can students engage actively with subject matter within the South African context? Put differently, how can students contribute to construction of knowledge? Statistics show that South Africa was undertaking approximately 0.5 percent of the world's scientific research in 1994, with the balance of output favoring social sciences and humanities rather than natural sciences. There is an obvious need to focus on knowledge construction in order to boost the country's research capacity. A key policy goal is therefore to equip all graduates with the skills and qualities needed for participation as citizens in a democratic society and as workers and professionals in the economy.

We suggest that African philosophy has the potential to make a positive contribution to university teaching in a democratic South Africa.

Higgs (2003) argues that an African philosophy can contribute to construction of empowering knowledge that enables communities in South Africa to participate in their own educational development. He further states that people cannot be empowered if they are locked into ways of thinking that work to oppress them; nor can they be empowered if they do not have access to those indigenous forms of knowledge that give them their identity as persons.

The importance of these indigenous forms of knowledge or knowledge systems was recognized in 1998 when the Portfolio Committee of Parliament instructed the Department of Arts, Culture, Science, and Technology to embark on formation of a policy and subsequent legislation on recognizing, promoting, and protecting indigenous knowledge systems in South Africa. The policy and legislation sought to legitimate indigenous knowledge systems on their own terms by creating an authoritative enabling environment for development and articulation of all domains of indigenous knowledge systems, including higher education. As a result, the question of the Africanization of the curriculum has become a dominant theme in the transformation of higher education in South Africa, with far-reaching consequences for the role of the university in South Africa, educational development of staff in universities, and the curriculum for teacher education.

Currently, a postgraduate degree (in most cases at least a master's degree) is required to teach at a university. Training for university teaching is conducted through departmental, faculty, or universitywide staff development programs. What is lacking though, is special emphasis on *ubuntu* (in traditional African morality, a concern with human welfare best captured in the concept of "humanism," which here refers to a philosophy that sees human needs, interests, and dignity as of fundamental importance and concern) and communalism. Yet there seems to be general acceptance of these prominent features of African society becoming part of Africanizing university curricula.

The philosophical underpinning of the emphasis on the importance of indigenous forms of knowledge in the South African context, especially as it relates to higher education, finds expression in what Masolo (in Chukwu, 2002) suggests as being the two aspects of the philosophical task that are truly typical of philosophizing in an African context: the quest for genuine knowledge, and integration of African experiences into a unified and coherent view. African philosophy should be able to respond to the problems and human conditions in modern Africa. It should also clarify the concepts, beliefs, and values that we hold, use, and live by, through sustained discussion and dialogue. It follows that an African philosophical perspective can assist in clarifying concepts and beliefs associated with higher education in an African context. Specifically, it assists us in rethinking higher education in accordance with the idea of an African university.

Higher education policies in South Africa link the university to concepts such as democracy, gender, knowledge and scholarship, quality, African languages, African orientation, identity, and cultural orientation. These concepts present challenges that have to be given serious attention because they have a direct bearing on the success of students.

NEW DIRECTIONS FOR HIGHER EDUCATION • DOI 10.1002/he

Vilakazi (2000) refers to the challenge and crisis facing African universities, suggesting that as producers of well-thought out and debated knowledge they must in our age become the dominant source of guiding light for society. Accordingly, universities in Africa must master the crisis, intellectually and scientifically, and demonstrate to society and to the continent the way out of the crisis. The crisis, according to Vilakazi, is that African universities have not lived up to the responsibility and challenge of becoming the guiding light to the continent and the societies within which they are located.

To live up to this challenge requires that the higher education sector and its constituent HEIs continuously examine themselves—their internal organization and their approaches to curriculum development and knowledge production—to monitor the extent of their economic, social, cultural, and intellectual contribution to (South) African society. At the national level, the HEQC reviews of programs serve as a guide to academics to adjust programs to meet minimum criteria for accreditation; this ensures that quality is built into curricula.

Maliyamkono (1994) suggests that higher education centers in Africa seem to be playing four main roles: educating high-level manpower through teaching and learning, development and application of new knowledge through research for the benefit of society, furnishing public service to society through consultancies and other community-oriented activities, and making higher education campuses centers of political force. Urch (in Maliyamkono, 1994) has identified five operational problems facing education (which we think have an impact on higher education) in Africa, in general: the African heritage (what to retain, modify, or replace), the colonial heritage, the language problem in schools, the dichotomy between education for self-reliance and education for technological and industrial advancement, and education for national unity.

In this regard, Husén (1994) observes that universities in Africa, Asia, and Latin America were often established according to European models. Graduates from these continents were sent to Europe and the United States for advanced degrees to produce indigenous faculty to replace expatriates. Those who studied abroad and were assigned teaching positions after completion of their studies quite naturally emulated the practices established at the institutions where they conducted their studies. As a result, curricula at universities in Third World countries have usually been patterned on European models. Husén then asserts that the Eurocentric system of university education has hampered universities in these countries in releasing endogenous creativity and seeking their cultural roots. There is thus a tension between the orientation toward indigenous values and problems on the one hand and addressing global problems on the other, a tension that can be alleviated or resolved only through communication across cultural boundaries.

New Directions for Higher Education • DOI 10.1002/he

In light of our sense of Africanness, what then are the implications for constructing an African discourse in a philosophy of higher education? What ought to be the purpose of higher education in an African context and within the framework of African philosophy?

Notwithstanding the diversity inherent in an African knowledge system, we identify two general themes in African philosophy, namely communalism and ubuntu. These two themes can be said to be pervasive in African philosophical thought in a socioethical sense in that they transcend the cultural, linguistic, and ethnic diversity of African peoples. In this light, it might be proposed that educating for communal life and ubuntu would be crucial to traditional African educational thought and practice.

Educating for life in the community would be rooted in what Mkabela and Luthuli (1997) note as a welfare concern, where the basis of communalism is giving priority to the community and respect for the person. It also involves sharing with and helping people. Higher educational discourse within this African frame of reference would help African people function in relation to one another in their communal tradition. Such a functioning would promote a collective effort directed ultimately at the good of the community. This collective effort would in turn be characterized by a spirit of ubuntu, which deems human need, interests, and dignity of fundamental importance and concern. For higher educational endeavors, this would mean that traditional African educational thought and practice would be directed at fostering humane people endowed with moral norms and virtues such as kindness, generosity, compassion, benevolence, courtesy, respect, and concern for others. In short, an African higher educational discourse would be fundamentally concerned with ubuntu in service to the community and personal well-being.

The emphasis on ubuntu and communalism points to a complex relationship between education and social development, which could be a key feature of a new South African citizenry. Students who graduate with an appreciation of these features can make a significant contribution to society because they have these "traditional" intellectual skills. Also, academics need to ensure that curricula reflect these values; it is about transforming what we actually teach students. Programs must be adapted to develop scientific skills and values that can deepen democracy. All of this means that the research agenda of universities will certainly have to be cognizant of these fundamental issues that are addressed within the context of African philosophy in coming to terms with the Africanization of the curriculum.

Emphasis on communalism and ubuntu in traditional African thought and experience also requires higher education in the African context to pay attention to interpersonal and cooperative skills. In this regard, Letseka (2000) argues that "certainly interpersonal skills have been shown to be an integral part of educating for ubuntu and the promotion of communally accepted and desirable moral norms and virtues" (p. 189).

NEW DIRECTIONS FOR HIGHER EDUCATION • DOI 10.1002/he

Traditional education in the African context has sought to instill desirable attitudes, dispositions, skills, and habits in the community by means of recounting the oral traditions of the community. A great deal of philosophical and educational material is, as Okeke (1982) notes, embedded in the oral traditions and customs of the people. An important aspect of traditional African education thought and practice is therefore concerned with teaching oral tradition as well as helping members of the community learn to use language creatively and effectively. According to Boateng (1990) and Fajana (1986), such learning is in essence a central feature in African educational practices because it is through oral traditions that much of the history of the community, as well as its values and beliefs, are passed on from one generation to the next. Consequently, oral tradition played an active part in the African's everyday life and was a vital educational force in supplying accounts of a group's origin and related precedents to present-day beliefs, actions, and codes of behavior. An educated person in an African context is, according to Fafunwa (1974), an individual who is "honest, respectable, skilled, [and] cooperative and [who] conforms to the social order of the day" (p. 20).

In this sense, traditional African educational thought and practice is characterized not only by its concern with the person but also by its interweaving of social, economic, political, cultural, and educational threads into a common tapestry. As a result, traditional education in Africa is distinguished by the importance attached to its collective and social nature, as well as its intimate tie with social and communal life. Higher education, then, in the traditional African setting, cannot, and indeed should not, be separated from life itself. It is a natural process by which members of the community gradually acquire skills, knowledge, and attitudes appropriate to life in their community—a higher education inspired by a spirit of ubuntu in service to the community.

References

Barnett, R. "Philosophy." In B. R. Clarke and G. Neave (eds.), The Encyclopedia of Higher Education. Vol. 3: Analytical Perspectives. New York and Oxford: Pergamon Press, 1992.

Boateng, F. "African Traditional Education: A Tool for Intergenerational Communication." In M. Asante and K. Asante (eds.), African Culture: Rhythms of Unity. Trenton: Africa World Press, 1990.

Chukwu, C. N. "African Philosophy: The Task of Addressing Contemporary Social Problems." In G. M. Presbey, D. Smith, P. A. Abuya, and O. Nyarwath (eds.), Thought and Practice in African Philosophy. Nairobi: Konrad Adenauer Foundation, 2002.

Council on Higher Education (CHE). Towards a New Higher Education Landscape: Meeting the Equity, Quality and Social Development Imperatives of South Africa in the 21st Century. Pretoria: CHE, Shape and Size of Higher Education Task Team, 2000.

Council on Higher Education (CHE). South African Higher Education in the First Decade of Democracy. Pretoria: CHE, 2004.

Department of Education. Education White Paper 3: A Programme for the Transformation of Higher Education. *Pretoria: Department of Education, 1997.*

Fafunwa, B. *A History of Education in Nigeria.* London: Allen and Unwin, 1974.

Fajana, A. "Traditional Methods of Education in Africa: The Yoruba Example." In J. Okpaku, A. Opubor, and B. Oloruntimehin (eds.), *The Arts and Civilization of Black and African Peoples. Vol. 6: Black Civilization and Pedagogy.* Lagos: Center for Black and African Arts and Civilization, 1986.

Higgs, P. "African Philosophy and the Transformation of Education Discourse in South Africa." *Journal of Education,* 2003, *30,* 5–22.

Husén, T. "The Idea of the University: Changing Roles, Current Crisis and Future Challenges." In T. Husén (ed.), *The Role of the University: A Global Perspective.* Tokyo: United Nations University, 1994.

Laurillard, D. "New Technologies, Students and the Curriculum: The Impact of Communications and Information Technology on Higher Education." In P. Scott (ed.), *Higher Education Re-formed.* (New Millennium Series.) London and New York: Falmer Press, 2000.

Letseka, M. "African Philosophy and Educational Discourse." In P. Higgs, N.C.G. Vakalisa, T. V. Mda, and N. T. Assie-Lumumba (eds.), *African Voices in Education.* Cape Town: Juta, 2000.

Maliyamkono, T. L. "Higher Education in Africa." In T. Husén (ed.), *The Role of the University: A Global Perspective.* Tokyo: United Nations University, 1994.

Ministry of Education. *National Plan for Higher Education.* Pretoria: Ministry of Education, 2001.

Mkabela, N. Q., and Luthuli, P. C. *Towards an African Philosophy of Education.* Pretoria: Kagiso, 1997.

Okeke, A. "Traditional Education in Igboland." In F. Ogbalu and E. Emenanjo (eds.), *Igbo, Language and Culture.* Ibadan: University Press, 1982.

Vilakazi, H. W. "The Problem of Education in Africa." In P. Higgs, N.C.G. Vakalisa, T. Mda, and N. T. Assie-Lumumba (eds.), *African Voices in Education.* Lansdowne: Juta, 2000.

PHILIP HIGGS *is professor in the School for Graduate Studies in the College of Human Sciences of the University of South Africa.*

BERTE VAN WYK *is professor of education policy studies at Stellenbosch University, South Africa.*

10

Two evaluation models were used in Brazil as tools for policies of higher education undertaken by two different administrations.

Changes in Brazilian Higher Education and Their Effects on the Enhancement of Teaching (1995–2005)

José Dias Sobrinho

Higher education in Brazil has passed through some important changes in the last ten years. Between 1995 and 2005, evaluation policies were used as a guideline for changes in pedagogical practices, in institutions and in the higher education system as a whole.

The official modernization policies that came into effect after 1995 aimed at surpassing some bureaucratic obstacles and a set of values both of which supposedly prevented Brazil from participating in the new worldwide reality of economic globalization. The new social demands are of a truly complex nature: rise of competition; new professional profiles, innovations, and transformations of the current capitalism state; and incremental efficiency and productivity.

Higher education policies established in the last ten years responded mainly to increased demand for opportunity for higher education. Thus it would be necessary to submit universities to a modernizing "shock"—in other words, relieve them from their bureaucratic excesses and weighed structures, make them function more effectively in economic terms, and broaden the educational market.

The main characteristics of the modernization undertaken in higher education are enormous expansion of institutions and the student population; drastic reduction of public resources leading to growth of the private

NEW DIRECTIONS FOR HIGHER EDUCATION, no. 133, Spring 2006 © Wiley Periodicals, Inc.
Published online in Wiley InterScience (www.interscience.wiley.com) • DOI: 10.1002/he.209

educational market and a pervasiveness of a mercantile mentality; some initiatives toward transnationalization; greater flexibility of the means combined with rigid control of the ends of higher education; and changes in the university's ethos.

Rise in Enrollment and Private Institutions

Although the developed countries have already experienced the transition to mass higher education, the Brazilian system still has not surpassed the elite regimen. Although the number of higher education students and institutions in Brazil grows consistently (especially after 1998), only about 10 percent of Brazilians between eighteen and twenty-four are actually enrolled in higher courses. Despite the fact that university enrollment has presented an annual growth of 12 percent in the current year, it is still far below the Latin American average, which is close to 20 percent. On the other hand, Brazil has developed the most solid and widest postgraduation and research system of all Latin America.

Brazilian higher education is quite recent. Some few isolated higher courses were established in the nineteenth century, but the two first Brazilian universities (São Paulo and Rio de Janeiro) emerged only in 1934 and 1935, respectively. In recent decades, many higher education institutions were established, although less than 10 percent of them fulfill university requirements.

The increase in enrollment and number of institutions observed in the last decade is especially due to expansion of the private sector, although a significant rise is also observed in the public system. In 2003, the number of higher education institutions in Brazil was 1,859, distributed as 163 universities (8.8 percent); 81 higher education centers (4.3 percent); 119 integrated colleges (6.4 percent); 1,403 colleges, schools, and institutes (75.5 percent); and 93 technological education centers (5.0 percent). The Brazilian higher education system is one of the world's most privatized. Participation in the private sector has been consistently growing over the last few years. Among the 900 higher education institutions in Brazil in 1997, 689 were private; in 2003, among 1,859 institutions 1,652 were private (88.9 percent). Among the private institutions, there are those that are profit-driven (78.8 percent) and those that are considered communitarian, philanthropic, or confessional (that is, religious) (21.2 percent) (INEP/MEC), 2004). Public institutions (11.1 percent of the total) are divided as follows: eighty-three federal institutions, sixty-five state institutions, and fifty-nine municipal institutions.

In 1970, there were 425,478 enrolled students; in 1996, 1,868,529; and in 2003, 3,887,022 (INEP/MEC, 2003), from which less than 30 percent were enrolled in public institutions (INEP/MEC, 2004). Thus 70 percent of Brazilian students pay tuition fees.

NEW DIRECTIONS FOR HIGHER EDUCATION • DOI 10.1002/he

Public Funding Crisis and Strengthening of Mercantile Ideology

Funding represents a central challenge to system expansion, to the economic and political crisis, and to the rising complexity of the knowledge and information society. This complex context has led to adoption of policies that facilitate expansion of the private supply of educational services and consolidation of the educational market. Education is seen as something that benefits the individual, not as a public good or a social right.

Diversification and Differentiation

New types of organizations emerged as a result of either increased demand for study placement or a strategy of fierce survival. New short-term courses emerged in areas where the market shows restriction and immediate demand; many of them have little in common with traditional academic concepts but are able to absorb the new groups of students (or "customers"). About 40 percent of Brazilian higher education institutions have fewer than five hundred students enrolled.

Trends in Transnational Accreditation

Interaction within supranational spaces, interdependence networks, intensification of intercultural understanding, and media modernization generate an important expansion of new fields of study that are of great market appeal and, in many cases, tied to virtual environments and new technologies. They also contribute to expansion of transnational educational companies and pedagogical innovations based on new technologies. Because internationalization requires quality comparability according to objective standards, as well as curricula and program compatibility, it encourages creation of international control mechanisms. With an ever growing trend toward internationalization of the educational market, regulation tends to be increasingly performed by transnational agencies.

These accreditation processes, in some cases operated by supranational agencies, generally replace institutional self-evaluation and more qualitative evaluation in general.

Evaluation and Control

Evaluation, with its strict and controlling regulatory nature, is central to the remodeling of higher education recently observed in Brazil thanks to its high potential to influence the crucial matter of funding for institutions, recognition of their social value, the scope of their autonomy, and consolidation of certain conceptions of educational and pedagogical practices. In the last ten years, two evaluation models have been set into practice.

NEW DIRECTIONS FOR HIGHER EDUCATION • DOI 10.1002/he

Between 1995 and 2002, the Brazilian government made use of evaluation mechanisms focused on results and performance. Quantification of outcomes supplied elements for establishing institutional rankings. The instruments adopted for evaluation and control during this period were the National Courses Examination and Analysis of Teaching Conditions.

The National Courses Examination, based on the assumption that the quality of a given course corresponds with the performance of its students, produced important effects on the general higher education configuration, on the pedagogical projects of institutions, and on the pedagogical mentality of professors and students. For many students and courses, obtaining a good ranking was the main objective. Thus the adopted strategy (especially on the part of private institutions with no long teaching tradition) consisted of reducing the curriculum to the content that might be on the test, and training students to obtain higher performance on the test.

Therefore a mechanical relation between education and learning was established, which simplified curricula, increased the distance between curriculum construction and the experience of professors and students, and led to the belief that curriculum definition must be induced by external agencies, holders of a supposedly good technique of test elaboration. Basically performed as control, it debilitated some efforts of self-evaluation and self-regulation in many Brazilian institutions.

Research was restricted to some few institutions of excellence, losing importance in comparison to technical market functionality.

According to recurrent criticism from within the university environment, these evaluation instruments reduced the quality of higher education professionals and led to disinterest of many teaching institutions for procedures, objectives, logics, and demands from the market field. Thus it is generally felt that they caused a weakening of university autonomy in relation to knowledge, apprenticeship, and freedom of inquiry, which are basic elements of public life and citizenship.

Since the government of President Lula da Silva came into power in 2003, a new Higher Education National Evaluation System (SINAES) is in force. The new evaluation model is not narrowed to test students' performance or check the minimum conditions for a course to work, but instead attempts to articulate the various dimensions (educative, social, administrative) of institutions and of higher education as a whole. The new model gives greater weight to institutional self-knowledge, with the objective of allowing institutions to construct more democratic and educative practices (Simons, 1987) that have greater social relevance. Apart from having the function of pedagogical and scientific improvement and institutional empowerment, the new evaluation model also gives the ministry of education information required for regulation of the higher education system and course accreditation. This system intends to encourage didactic-pedagogical practices, attitudes, and innovation on the part of university professors in agreement with the political and economic projects of the country, to deepen their democratic values, stimulate development of critical and investigative attitudes in students, stimulate exercise of citizenship and active participation in social life, valorize personal experience in constructing and attaining knowledge, and elaborate a curriculum in agreement with new ways of obtaining knowledge and with the demands of the current society.

There is no evaluation instrument applied throughout the country exclusively to professors. However, many institutions evaluate their professors. In such cases, these instruments are associated with promotion programs or the idea of teaching effectiveness and are restricted to an opinion questionnaire, using only a few teaching and knowledge comprehension items. In addition, many institutions promote valuable institutional evaluation experiences that have benefited the professors' critical reflection processes in relation to their teaching practices (Stenhouse, 2002; Schön, 1983; Liston and Zeichner, 1993) and in relation to development of the conditions, values, and attitudes that would contribute to professional and institutional strengthening.

New Proposals and Attempts in Progress

With changes in government, since 2003 some important advances in Brazilian higher education have been observed. The minister of education has emphatically declared his opposition to the vision of higher education as a service or merchandise to be regulated by the World Trade Organization. In July 2005, he released for public discussion the third version of his proposal for higher education reform. The three main aspects of the reform are (1) linking higher education with the project of the nation (a new model for development), (2) democratization of higher education, and (3) constitution of rules that promote continuous empowerment of the system and hinder the mercantilization of education.

Several affirmative policies are implemented, especially those that produce greater social inclusion.

The reform seeks to recover an important aspect of the university's ethos, one that grants a clearly public and social meaning to university teaching: formation aimed at social life, the participation of actors of the institutional community in exercise of citizenship and social responsibility.

Brazil has a perverse history of exclusion of the poor and ethnic minorities, particularly Afro descendants. Therefore the ministry of education considers extending some policies that have granted access that the poor have to public schools to include higher education institutions. Beyond reserves of quotas, they are also granted scholarships in order to guarantee their permanence and better conditions for attending a higher course.

Fewer than 30 percent of the Brazilian college students are now enrolled in public institutions. The goal of the current government is to reach 40 percent of the total of students in the present decade.

Initiatives and Challenges to Reinforce Pedagogical Formation

With growth in the number of courses and students, the roster of university professors also increased. In 1994, there were 141,482 professors; in 2003 this number increased to 254,153 (INEP/MEC, 2004). The rise in the number of courses, students, and professors had an important impact on university teaching. Although public institutions essentially hire only Ph.D. professors, and although not all professors have had higher education teaching formation, new and small private institutions are regularly hiring lower-level professionals, many with no pedagogical formation and with no improvement in conditions while working.

The formation of professors for all teaching levels takes place at universities. They offer graduate and postgraduate courses and develop research in a variety of fields—at university centers, integrated colleges, higher education schools, and institutes. Nonuniversity institutions produce no research at all; according to recurrent criticism from many professors, many of them offer formation with lower academic requirements. Unlike universities, the teaching in these new and small private institutions is more aimed at attainment of good results in evaluations and adaptation to the professional profiles required in the labor market than at permanent qualification of professors and articulation between teaching and research.

Along with a lack of continuing professional development and the absence of rewards for conduct of research, some differences may also be verified in the professors' employment contracts.

The contracts from the new private institutions follow the employment laws and norms elaborated by supporting companies. These companies define hiring-and-firing criteria, and above all they consider the results of evaluation processes, official accreditation guidelines, and the logic of the market. In many cases, in the new and small private institutions contracts are "made flexible" (that is, temporary, outsourced, no progression perspective, and so on). In public institutions, teaching is more clearly defined, and present-day promotion criteria are based on academic merit. In these institutions, most professors are hired in full-time positions and need to dedicate themselves to teaching and research. They must demonstrate intellectual productivity and are subject to evaluation from their academic peers. In federal institutions, teaching evaluations are sometimes linked to merit pay, as is the case in some other countries. However, a professor from a public institution is rarely fired.

Postgraduation: Formation of Higher Education Professors

Since the decade of the 1960s, the Brazilian postgraduate program has been aimed at forming professors and higher-level researchers with the objective of fulfilling the qualitative and quantitative demands of the higher education

NEW DIRECTIONS FOR HIGHER EDUCATION • DOI 10.1002/he

system in order to develop the scientific research required for national development in all sectors.

The Brazilian postgraduate system is composed of *lato sensu* courses (specialization, improvement, and professional updating, currently 350,000 students) and of *stricto sensu* courses (master's of science and Ph.D. degree). There are about 1,600 master's of science and Ph.D. programs with 100,000 students, 86 percent of them in public institutions, especially in the southeast of the country. It is important to observe that the public universities (federal and state institutions) and some catholic universities are the institutions providing the highest and most significant contribution to research in general and to formation and qualification of professors.

In Brazil, approximately 10,000 Ph.D. and 23,000 M.S. degrees are obtained annually. Most of these postgraduate students dedicate themselves to teaching and researching in universities and other higher education institutions. Among the 254,153 university professors, 89,288 have an M.S. degree and 54,497 have a Ph.D., according to data from 2003 (www.capes.gov.br; INEP/MEC, 2004). There are several central services linked to the ministry of education that support this system with guidelines, evaluations, funding, and pedagogical support. Moreover, many associations and forums promote debate, organize conferences, and accomplish much interinstitutional research. These associations include the National Association of Postgraduation and Research in Education, the National Association for the Formation of Education Professionals, and the Brazilian Engineering Teaching Association, among others. There are also some well-known journals that support the professional development of professors.

Postgraduate courses are the main instance of formation and qualification of Brazilian university professors, but not all of them develop programs exclusively aimed at forming professors for the university teaching. Except for postgraduate courses in the education area, all others deepen their knowledge in their respective areas and acquire abilities in research, but not in teaching. This disparity between formation aimed at research and for-mation for pedagogical practice leads to the common idea that being a content expert is sufficient for being a good professor.

Postgraduate courses in the education area are mainly aimed at forming higher education professors and researchers in education and at development of educational research. The increasing number of education schools, consolidation of their scientific production, the requirement of an M.S. degree and a Ph.D., and progression in one's university career are some of the reasons for the quantitative and qualitative growth of the seventy M.S. and Ph.D. programs in the education area.

Many postgraduate courses in other areas (medicine, dentistry, administration, and so on) have included subjects for formation of higher education professors in their study plans.

Universities have created mechanisms to support teaching such as advisory services to professors; teaching-qualification training programs; financing of innovative teaching projects, discussion groups, and seminars on teaching; supervised training courses for formation of new professors; and institutional evaluations to diagnose the main teaching and apprenticeship problems and improve knowledge of effective teaching practices.

The ministry of education also develops many programs related to formation of university professors. Some programs developed by the CAPES/ MEC (Higher Level Personnel Improvement Coordination) deserve emphasis: Oriented Teaching in Higher Education (teaching activity that is obligatory for scholarship holders and supervised by the orienting professor); the Teaching Qualification Program (supports qualification of professors from private institutions); and the CAPES Website, which allows access to three thousand scientific journals from main international research centers.

In short, despite considerable difficulties such as loss of social status, low salaries, mass school registration, fragmentation of the higher education system and formation structures, shrinking budgets, the knowledge explosion, tensions, and conceptual and political contradictions, a set of ideas and projects aimed at enhancing formation and qualification of higher education professors is being developed by the federal government, by the state education bureaus, and above all by the community of professors themselves. They are aimed at competence in the knowledge area; capacity of critical reflection on Brazil and the world community; continued professional development (seminars, workshops, advisory pedagogical services, scientific journals, and so on); innovation and new technologies; qualification of postgraduate students for higher-level teaching; valorization of pedagogical research; evaluation of teaching practice; and reflection on the meaning of formation.

In Brazil, demand for higher education teaching is shaped by the historical, social, cultural, and educational needs of the country, insufficiency of funds, regional diversity, and the vastness of the territory. This diversity impairs elaboration of national strategies aimed at enhancing formation of students and future professors, qualification of teachers, and higher education teaching: "Globalization requires a more flexible teaching organization, the overcoming of inflexible disciplinary and departmental structures and a more interactive and reflective attitude. While acquisition of specific knowledge is still important for the solution of problems, a wider and long-term view would suggest that more complex epistemologies, reflective attitudes and interdisciplinary practices acquire greater relevance" (Dias Sobrinho, 2005, p. 234). Perhaps more than in countries from the First World, the university professor in Brazil, along with an area of academic specialization, needs to have a sensibility for the political and social matters of Brazilian reality.

References

Dias Sobrinho, J. *Dilemas da educação superior no mundo globalizado: Sociedade do conhecimento ou economia do conhecimento?* São Paulo: Casa do Psicólogo, 2005.

Instituto Nacional de Estudos e Pesquisas Educacionais Anísio Teixeira (INEP/MEC). *Censo da Educação Superior 2003.* Brasília, D.F.: Ministério da Educação, 2003.

Instituto Nacional de Estudos e Pesquisas Educacionais Anísio Teixeira (INEP/MEC). *Censo da Educação Superior 2003.* Brasília, D.F.: Ministério da Educação, 2004.

Liston, D., and Zeichner, K. M. *Formación del profesorado y condiciones sociales de la escolarización.* Madrid: Morata, 1993.

Schön, D. A. *The Reflective Practitioner.* New York: Basic Books, 1983.

Simons, H. *Getting to Know Schools in a Democracy: The Politics and Process of Evaluation.* London: Falmer Press, 1987.

Stenhouse, L. "The Teacher as Researcher." In A. Pollard (ed.), *Reading for Reflective Teaching.* London: Continuum, 2002.

JOSÉ DIAS SOBRINHO is professor in the State University of Campinas (UNICAMP) and the University of Sorocaba (UNISO), Brazil, where he teaches and conducts research on the subject of higher education evaluation. He is also founder and editor of the journal Avaliação *(Evaluation), which publishes articles on the same subject.*

NEW DIRECTIONS FOR HIGHER EDUCATION • DOI 10.1002/he

11

The level of funding made available for pedagogical innovation, a function of external policy context, is important but not sufficient for effecting lasting change in higher education teaching.

Comparing Approaches Taken in Different Countries

Carolin Kreber

The main purpose of this volume has been to highlight national differences in higher education policy geared directly at university teaching and learning in an era that is generally recognized as one of drastic and rapid change, resource constraints, and intensified performance accountability. To this end, the previous chapters served to document the policy approaches nine countries have taken to enhancement of teaching and learning within an increasingly complex higher education environment. This last chapter concludes with an attempt at identifying what can be learned from the documented experiences of these nine countries.

External Influences on Enhancement of Teaching and Learning

Six main observations can be readily made in light of the preceding chapters. First, all nine countries have higher education systems in place that consist of traditional universities offering undergraduate and postgraduate degrees on the one hand and, on the other, more vocationally oriented institutions (often polytechnics) that received university status in recent years or further education colleges that also offer higher education programs in selected subject areas, usually confined to the undergraduate level. Rice's insight that the diversity of institutions in the United States has contributed significantly

NEW DIRECTIONS FOR HIGHER EDUCATION, no. 133, Spring 2006 © Wiley Periodicals, Inc.
Published online in Wiley InterScience (www.interscience.wiley.com) • DOI: 10.1002/he.210

to the quality of teaching (see Chapter Two) is worth remembering here. In the United Kingdom, for example, the strongest support for teaching has come from the ranks of the newer universities, which traditionally have been more teaching-oriented, and in Canada teaching is much more highly valued at colleges or university-colleges offering university transfer programs. Furthermore, Donald observes in Chapter Three that smaller universities in Canada value teaching more highly than larger (and typically more research-intensive) universities. As the U.S. and UK experience shows, pedagogical projects launched by smaller institutions, especially when combined with an adequate level of funding, can eventually have a profound influence on pedagogy also in larger and more research-intensive institutions.

Second, it is apparent that internationally the past decade has experienced a trend toward greater performance accountability within the higher education sector combined with stronger external quality assurance systems, and increasingly cyclical accreditation of programs or institutions has become more common. Despite such greater external controls, in many countries universities are rewarded for strengthening their internal quality assurance systems in exchange for public funds. However, the case of Brazil illustrates how transnational agencies increasingly regulate institutions by requiring comparability of standards and programs to advance internationalization, thus mitigating efforts aimed at serious institutional self-evaluation and self-regulation. For example, when in the period 1995–2002 the quality of courses in Brazil was measured on the basis of student performance, this policy led universities to "teach to the test" to secure funds. Verhesschen, describing the situation in Flanders, raises similar concerns in arguing that demands for external accountability may discourage institutions from engaging in serious self-evaluation because it would be disadvantageous in the present policy climate to admit to areas that may benefit from improvement. Instead, institutions are encouraged to portray themselves in the best possible light to secure funding. It should also be noted (albeit in passing) that quality assurance is not necessarily uniform within one country either. In Canada, for example, where education falls within the realm of provincial rather than federal legislation and responsibility, each province has its own procedures for quality control and approval of new programs (see Chapter Three). Cyclical program reviews are common practice in the province of Ontario, but by contrast the province of Alberta at present still relies more heavily on internal reviews and requires external accreditation of new programs. Still, all Canadian universities need to be accredited at the federal level, namely by the Association of Universities and Colleges of Canada (AUCC).

Third, public or government support of higher education has declined over the years while at the same time demands for institutional performance accountability have been raised. Some countries—for example, Australia and the United Kingdom—have begun to separate funds for teaching from

NEW DIRECTIONS FOR HIGHER EDUCATION • DOI 10.1002/he

funds for research, and there is growing evidence in most countries that in the future the quality of teaching will have even greater implications for how institutions are funded. For example, as Lindblom-Ylänne points out for the Finnish context, at institutions where the faculty is expected to undergo frequent cyclical program reviews of the quality of their teaching this already indirectly affects future funding in cases where such funding is dependent on the number of degrees conferred. The reasoning here is that if the quality of teaching is not high and students do not receive the support they need, their pace of study is being slowed down, some may even drop out, and consequently fewer degrees are conferred in a given year. This situation certainly is not unique to Finland but constitutes a significant issue at all institutions that are required to undergo frequent program quality evaluations.

Fourth, the Bologna process in Europe—requiring drastic restructuring of programs from a two-year- to a three-year-cycle degree structure (bachelor's, master's, and doctoral degrees) so as to enhance student mobility as well as economic competitiveness, combined with tighter timelines within which to complete a program of study, detailed articulation of learning outcomes, and greater emphasis on student-focused inquiry-based approaches to teaching—has had a profound influence also on the professional development needs of university departments and their faculty. "Bologna" therefore serves as an excellent example of how the external higher education policy environment can be a driver for policies specifically geared at enhancement of university teaching and learning.

Interestingly, perhaps not all European countries have been equally successful to date in assisting universities and their staff in the transition period Bologna requires. Though professional development of university teachers is clearly linked to Bologna in Germany as well, Webler observes in Chapter Six that German academics did not receive adequate preparation for developing new curricula, let alone for serving as accreditors of new bachelor's programs that needed to be developed to meet the objectives associated with the Bologna process. Consequently, newly revised curricula continue to be teacher-focused and content (input)-driven; material that used to be studied over the course of ten semesters now has been crammed into eight, thereby implicitly encouraging students to forgo a deep and inquiry-based approach to their learning (precisely, of course, the opposite of what Bologna is meant to achieve). As Lindblom-Ylänne describes in Chapter Seven, Helsinki solved this problem by deliberately employing a pool of staff with broad educational development experience to assist departments in their efforts at pedagogical innovation and curricula change.

Fifth, there seems to be a subtle yet notable difference between the chapters detailing countries with already strong economically developed systems and those of countries with less strong (but rapidly improving) economically developed systems in what the authors recognize as their higher education sector's most pressing and significant goals. All the countries remark on the importance of a strong higher education system to strengthen the economy, but post-apartheid South Africa and Brazil in particular highlight the need to link higher education to the development project of the nation. They are skeptical of internalization and trading of educational services and argue for a curriculum that is more soundly based on the needs of the country. Next to furthering the country's economic development—for example, by boosting its research capacity and emphasizing employability of graduates—it is interesting that they also emphasize as a major role of higher education support for the country's social and political development. Students, so they argue, need to acquire skills that allow them to fully participate in society not only as workers but also as citizens. What appears unique, therefore, about both the chapter on South Africa and the one on Brazil is that the authors highlight the various responsibilities associated with the role of the university, and by extension the role of the university professor in particular. Though there is perhaps less to report in these countries with respect to specific approaches taken to enhance the pedagogical expertise of teachers in higher education, it is indeed refreshing to see that the authors seem exceptionally reflective about the purposes of higher education in their country.

Furthermore, countries with considerably poorer rates of higher education participation (Brazil, South Africa, but also Australia) not surprisingly stress the democratization of higher education and call for greater social inclusion and access to public universities. This is of particular interest in Brazil, where most of the higher education system is privatized and where students have to pay fees at these private (and more vocationally oriented) institutions. Though higher education in Australia is considered public—note, however, that in Australia as elsewhere delivery of programs through private providers has drastically increased—rising tuition fees in some programs led to tension between higher education perceived as a private benefit and higher education perceived as a public good.

Sixth, all nine countries have some measures in place that support academic staff in their teaching role, but the extent to which these are overtly linked to larger policy initiatives or constitute actual professional development "programs" varies considerably from one country to the next.

Europe. As the chapters for Finland, Flanders, and Germany illustrated, "Bologna" (a process aimed at a common area of higher education policy in Europe) has brought with it both huge opportunities and challenges with respect to academic staff development. Both the University of Helsinki and the University of Leuven have responded by developing an institutionwide agenda centered on "student-focused research-based learning" and "guided independent learning," respectively; staff, and groups of staff members, can apply for funding to experiment with innovative projects within their department. In Germany, some states (for example, Baden-Württemberg and

Bavaria) have begun to follow the British example by offering courses for academic staff in order to prepare them for their teaching roles. Such programs are mandatory at present only in Bavaria (where they are based on 120 contact hours), but Webler observes that many new staff feel a moral obligation or responsibility to be better prepared for their teaching role (despite the fact that teaching still counts rather little in hiring decisions at German universities). A new development in Germany is also that teachers now can be rewarded for their teaching excellence by receiving merit pay—something unheard of only a few years ago. Similar practices in other countries such as Sweden (Roxa and Olsson, 2005) suggest that it is not the amount of money that is the motivating factor for most faculty (which typically is very modest) but the symbolic value they attribute to such rewards.

South Africa. Higgs and van Wyk observe that in South Africa staff have the opportunity to participate in departmental, faculty, or university-wide professional development initiatives, but there seems to be no national agenda or explicit policy objectives associated with such initiatives. As with the university curricula offered to students, the authors criticize these institutional professional development initiatives for not focusing on *ubuntu*—that is, on human need, interest, and dignity directed at fostering humane people endowed with certain moral norms and virtues such as kindness, generosity, compassion, benevolence, courtesy, respect, and concern for others (see Higgs and van Wyk, Chapter Nine). As such, these professional development initiatives do little by way of supporting staff in the most significant aspect of their work: teaching according to a truly South African philosophy. Such a philosophy would place ubuntu and "communalism" at the heart of what it means to be educated and thereby connect a concern for the person directly with the country's social, economic, political, and cultural needs. The authors do not mention any funding or other type of reward associated with the quality of higher education teaching, though they note, as do all our contributors, that general funding for higher education is increasingly performance-driven. The new Higher Education Quality Committee in South Africa accredits programs and audits institutions, for example.

Brazil. In Brazil, the very idea of professional development for university teachers is inextricably and closely linked to the research role of faculty. As Sobrinho illustrates in Chapter Ten, academics receive professional development by taking postgraduate courses in their area of specialization, and it is this postgraduate specialization that qualifies them to teach. Postgraduate courses in education or pedagogy are also available, but as one might expect they are meant for those who wish to teach in faculties of education. Overall, it would seem that in Brazil there is no real national movement in relation to enhancement of teaching and learning that is geared toward pedagogical preparation of staff; the traditional notion that "those who are experts in the field are also well prepared to teach it" features prominently. Nevertheless, Brazilian universities have some mechanisms in

place to support new teachers. There is some financing of innovative projects, discussion groups and seminars, and other induction programs. Perhaps more important, evaluation policies introduced recently under a new
government pay greater attention to fostering critical thinking skills, investigative approaches, and citizenship and consequently can be seen as initiatives directly linked to enhancement of teaching quality. Moreover,
democratization of the Brazilian higher education system is now an explicit
policy objective.

United States. In Chapter Two, Rice speaks of a "pedagogical revolution" that has taken hold in the United States over the past decade and at-
tributes it to evolving interest in research on how students learn. The
prestigious National Research Council and the National Science Foundation
(NSF) have been particularly influential in the United States in promoting
the idea that student learning is a phenomenon that can be studied and
indeed needs to be better understood in order to improve the quality of
teaching. The Center for the Integration of Research, Teaching, and
Learning (CIRTL) of the NSF has for many years involved graduate students
in projects aimed at better understanding the multiple links between the
structure of the subject matter and student learning tasks, and their implications for teaching. In the United States the idea of the "scholarship of
teaching," first proposed by the late Ernest Boyer (1990), has been further
promoted by both the former American Association for Higher Education
(AAHE) and the Carnegie Foundation for the Advancement of Teaching. In
the late 1990s, the latter launched the very successful Carnegie Academy
for the Scholarship of Teaching and Learning (CASTL). Though the academy advocates a "broad tent conceptualization" of the scholarship of teaching and learning (Huber and Hutchings, 2005) and as such does not see it
exclusively as pedagogical research in the discipline, it seems fair to say that
the academy encourages and supports pedagogical curiosity and inquiry on
the part of academic staff aimed at better understanding and supporting the
learning of their students, prepares faculty for this task through regular
group meetings and seminars, and promotes dissemination of insights gained
from these projects within the academic community. To fully appreciate the
U.S. context, it is important to note that large private foundations for a long
time now have made money available for advancement of education in the
form of competitive grants, with the resulting pedagogical innovations also
gradually infiltrating larger and traditionally more research-oriented institutions, on a scale that has been unknown by its neighbor to the north.

Canada. As Donald observes with respect to Canada in Chapter Three,
the concept of the scholarship of teaching and learning has taken hold there
too in recent years, as evidenced for example by presentations at the annual
meeting of the national Society for Teaching and Learning in Higher
Education (STLHE); however, there has been substantially less financial support for such projects than, for example, in the United States. The Canadian

Social Sciences and Humanities Research Council (SSHRC), though supporting research in education, does so only in exceptional cases—namely, if the proposed program of research is perceived to advance our knowledge of the field. The council does not therefore explicitly encourage context-specific forms of inquiry. This means projects that do get funded after a process of rigorous peer review are typically those proposed by experts in the field of education who can link their topic to larger concepts or issues in the field of learning, and not by faculty from other disciplines who are motivated to experiment with educational innovations with the goal of improving teaching and learning within their given contexts (personal experience as an external reviewer of grant proposals for the Social Sciences and Humanities Research Council of Canada, 2005). Although SSHRC would seem to be the obvious source of funding for projects aimed at the scholarship of teaching and learning (particularly now that the Canadian government is committed to investing more substantially in research), the underlying problem in Canada appears to be that to date academic staff have not received adequate training for carrying out such important work (and many will not be easily convinced that they need it).

Canada Compared to the United States, the United Kingdom, and Australia. Just as in the United States, Australia, and the United Kingdom, many of Canada's universities have small centers in place whose mandate is to support learning and teaching on campus; however, the extent to which they focus on the scholarship of teaching and learning varies greatly. Note that there is also in Canada no Carnegie Foundation or other private foundations as in the United States and no Higher Education Academy as in the United Kingdom, let alone no funding of the scale that, as Smith reports in Chapter Five, the Higher Education Funding Council for England makes available (for example, through its recently launched Centres for Excellence in Teaching and Learning, or the Teaching Quality Enhancement Fund, including the well-funded National Teaching Fellowships); nor is there a national institute for learning and teaching that supports national teaching fellowships and administers a Learning and Teaching Performance Fund, as Dearn reports in Chapter Four with respect to Australia (the Carrick Institute for Learning and Teaching in Higher Education). The Society for Teaching and Learning in Higher Education has been quite active for well over two decades and is an important forum in Canada for faculty to share ideas, educational innovations, and insights gained from pedagogical inquiry (typically conducted on a small scale and without external funding but at times supported through internal institutional grants). The society supports itself through membership fees. Many years ago, the society also introduced a National Teaching Award (known as the 3M Award), which is held in high regard, but the award exclusively rewards past excellence of staff, does not explicitly support further inquiry into teaching and learning or educational innovation, and (as would be expected) is associated with no funding comparable to that of the National Teaching Fellowship Scheme in the United Kingdom and Australia. Donald perceives emergence of the scholarship of teaching and learning as a promising initiative that may encourage further research on the instructional methods needed that would help students to engage in higher-order learning, but she cautions that what exactly is meant by "scholarship" by those who presently advocate the "scholarship of teaching" still needs to be seen. In comparison to other countries, it is also worth noting that though Canada has witnessed annual ranking of its universities for many years (published by *Maclean's* weekly news magazine), the criteria tend to focus more on research than on teaching, and the results are not linked to funding—which is in direct contrast to Australia, where several performance criteria in relation to teaching and learning are used to determine future funding of institutions.

As already noted, a major contextual factor and driver in policies directed at pedagogical innovation is the amount of government and other funding made available for this purpose. In Europe commitment to the Bologna process, specifically the changes in program structure and curricula that this common policy arena entails, has sparked several initiatives with respect to development of staff and teaching departments. The amount of government funding made available for enhancement of teaching quality in both Australia and the United Kingdom, as well as that provided through private foundations in the United States, is certainly "jealousy-inducing" to those who do not have access to resources of a similar scope but still hope to encourage their staff and departments to engage in pedagogical innovation and better understanding of student learning. It needs to be stressed, however, that enormous levels of funding in some countries have been made available in a context of increased performance accountability. In both Australia and Britain, funds for research have been separated from funds for teaching, and the dreaded Research Assessment Exercise places further pressure on institutions in these countries to demonstrate their quality on that plane. Yet performance accountability, as was shown, has increased globally. What then can be learned from the experience of these countries?

What Can Administrators Learn?

The previous case studies (particularly those of the United Kingdom, Australia, and the United States, but also the various initiatives in Europe) demonstrate that innovation in teaching can and will happen if adequate resources are made available. However, as many of the contributors point out, merely making funds available is clearly not sufficient. Pedagogical innovation and enhancement of teaching are directly linked to faculty being granted the time required to engage seriously with their professional development. It follows that institutions need to find ways to support rather than penalize staff who may not publish for some time while engaged in educational projects. Furthermore, as colleagues in Europe as well as in Britain suggest, a major concern at present is that it remains unclear what will happen once existing levels of funding run out. Can the innovations be sustained, or will they disappear as funds decline? Many countries therefore understand the need to disseminate good practice more widely, not only within and across departments but also across institutions.

Further, in relation to the issue of sustainability, it seems particularly worth mentioning that many countries have begun to recognize the importance of supporting departments rather than individuals in their development and to encourage staff collaboration and commitment to specific projects aimed at enhancing departmental teaching quality. Funding for institutions is often linked to development of institutional learning and teaching strategies (an institutionwide plan that lends guidance on how teaching quality is maintained and enhanced), and these learning and teaching strategies in turn constitute a meaningful framework for departments to propose and develop innovations that comply with the strategy. The universities of Helsinki and Leuven, for example, have quite successfully introduced schemes that allow departments to apply for funding to engage in innovation. Though this funding is on a much smaller scale than, for example, in the United Kingdom or Australia, the point to consider is that in order to enhance the student learning experience funding should not be concentrated exclusively in the hands of individual faculty (though such funding does have its place) because this could lead to many well-intended but isolated projects that may never become firmly integrated into the departmental curriculum. Note as well that there is a difference between encouraging innovation and rewarding past excellence. There is nothing inherently wrong with rewarding either individuals or departments for their past achievements; such practice provides little incentive for departments to improve further, nor (and much more important) does it address the real problem, which is, of course, the still-underachieving departments (or individuals). This is a point that Australia in particular may need to consider, given the $250 million Learning and Teaching Performance Fund intended to reward institutions that already do well.

It would indeed appear, at least in most countries reviewed here, that teaching is much more on the agenda today than even a few years ago (as Smith observes for the UK context); yet there continues to be a clear separation of research and teaching, with far greater emphasis being placed on research productivity than teaching quality—particularly, of course, at large research-intensive institutions. At elite institutions, performing adequately at teaching is still seen as sufficient, while being perceived as outstanding at research is the really significant criterion of excellence. Surely, in the United Kingdom, for example, the Quality Assurance Agency's cyclical institutional reviews of teaching quality (and National Student Surveys) are taken seriously, and considerable amounts of staff time are devoted to it also at elite institutions such as Oxford, the London School of Economics, and Edinburgh (in the present climate of performance accountability no institution, regardless of its research prowess, can afford to be perceived as performing poorly at teaching!).

However, there is no initiative in Britain that is viewed as having such far-reaching consequences as the Research Assessment Exercise (RAE). When much of an institution's funding (and national and international reputation) is linked directly to research productivity and quality, despite greater attention being paid to teaching quality than in the past, it assumes only secondary status. The upcoming 2008 RAE in the United Kingdom will consider pedagogical research in the disciplines, but it remains to be seen to what extent the submitted work will meet the criteria of the selection panels. The general sentiment across the United Kingdom is that staff engagement in pedagogical disciplinary research is *discouraged* by the RAE rather than encouraged. As with Canada, to date the United Kingdom has no measures in place for preparing staff to carry out pedagogical inquiry in the disciplines. The newly established Higher Education Academy recently launched a research and evaluation scheme aimed at encouraging more research on student learning, but only 2 percent of all submitted proposals were funded in this first competition (http://www.heacademy.ac.uk/researchprojects.htm). Surely, interest in the scheme was far greater than anticipated and funding simply was too scarce to be distributed across all applications, but the very fact that most project grants went to a handful of well-known scholars in the field speaks to most regular staff not having received adequate preparation in how to write grant proposals for pedagogical projects, let alone in how to carry out such research projects. Most would agree with Donald's observation in Chapter Three that more high-quality research is needed on how students learn and can be supported in their learning, but few recognize the need to adequately prepare faculty for this work. Indeed, much can be learned from the Carnegie Foundation's CASTL program in the United States, which explicitly introduces staff to the challenges and rewards that engaging in the scholarship of teaching and learning entail.

Many contributors point out that despite increased performance accountability with respect to teaching, teaching still counts rather little when it comes to hiring decisions. Individual institutions have begun to invite teaching portfolios as part of the application package, but the extent to which they carry weight in the decision-making process is unclear. Though some institutions offer comprehensive professional development programs for inexperienced staff, and in some jurisdictions participation in these programs is mandatory (for example, Bavaria and the United Kingdom), participation is not necessarily an advantage when it comes to hiring. However, the success and long-term effects of such initiatives (designing portfolios, participating in professional development programs, contributing educational innovations, conducting pedagogical inquiry, and so on) will be limited unless faculty perceive that their efforts are both recognized and rewarded by the institution.

What Can Faculty Developers Learn from the Experiences of These Countries?

To become a stronger player with respect to teaching quality enhancement on campus, faculty developers are advised to influence the institutional strategic plan in relation to teaching and learning and gear their development programs toward encouraging departments to develop context-specific initiatives that support the overall strategy. For example, if senior administrators can be convinced that the quality of teaching is enhanced as staff acquire deeper understanding of how students learn, the need for academic staff development to be informed by research on student learning and the need for faculty to be adequately prepared for their teaching role through participation in programs designed for that purpose can be written directly into the strategy. As part of the preparation program, faculty can be introduced not only to the latest research on learning and related "tips" or implications for teaching but also to approaches suitable to helping them carry out research projects themselves that are aimed at better understanding how their own students learn. Such programs should involve discipline-specific components (see in particular Chapters Five and Seven) and not be aimed exclusively at inexperienced faculty but instead provide opportunities for continuous professional development of all staff.

References

Boyer, E. *Scholarship Reconsidered.* Washington, D.C.: Carnegie Foundation, 1990.

Huber, M. T., and Hutchings, P. *The Advancements of Learning: Building the Teaching Commons. The Carnegie Foundation Report on the Scholarship of Teaching and Learning.* (Carnegie Foundation for the Advancement of Teaching.) San Francisco: Jossey-Bass, 2005.

Roxa, T., and Olsson, T. "The Case of Lund University." Presentation at Learning and Teaching Forum titled Alternative Career Paths and Rewards for Teaching: Sharing Experiences and Envisioning Alternatives, held at University of Edinburgh, Scotland, Dec. 20, 2005.

CAROLIN KREBER *is director of the Centre for Teaching, Learning, and Assessment at the University of Edinburgh, where she is also professor of teaching and learning in higher education in the Department of Higher and Community Education.*

NEW DIRECTIONS FOR HIGHER EDUCATION • DOI 10.1002/he

INDEX

Academic Freedom, 15–16

Academic Revolution, The (Jenks and Riesman), 16

Accountability: in Australia, 39; in Canada, 23, 25–27, 28; in Flanders, 79, 80, 102; intensified performance, 101, 102, 108, 110; in South Africa, 82, 105; trends toward greater, 8; in United Kingdom, 46–48, 51; in United States, 16–17

Accreditation: in Australia, 33, 38; in Brazil, 94, 96; criteria for, in Canada, 25–26; in Finland, 66; in Flanders, 75, 77, 80; in Germany, 55, 57, 60, 103; in South Africa, 84, 85, 87; transnational, trends in, 93, 102; in United Kingdom, 45; in United States, 16–18

Adelman, C., 25, 30

African philosophy, 85–89

Alberta, Canada, 27, 102

Altbach, P. G., 5, 10, 17, 22

American Association for Higher Education, 18, 21, 106

American Association of University Professors, 15

Arbeitsgruppe Hochschulforschung (Workgroup Research on HE), University of Konstanz, Germany, 58

Aronowitz, S., 6, 10

Ashwin, P., 68, 70

Assessment, 16–18, 24, 26, 27, 28, 34, 38, 40, 44, 45, 46, 50, 63, 68, 69, 75, 77, 84

Assessment Forum, 18

Association of American Colleges, 15

Association of American Colleges and Universities, 19

Association of American Universities, 24

Association of Universities and Colleges of Canada (AUCC), 24, 25, 26, 27, 28, 30, 31, 102

Australia, 1, 2, 33–41, 102, 104, 107, 108, 109

Australian Awards for University Teaching, 40

Australian Higher Education Quality Assurance Framework, 38, 39

Australian Qualifications Framework (AQF), 38

Australian Universities Quality Agency (AUQA), 38

Australian Universities Teaching Committee (AUTC), 40

Australian Vice-Chancellors' Committee (AVCC), 34, 35, 41

Axelrod, P. D., 7, 10

Banta, T., 27, 31

Barnett, R., 85, 89

Bavaria, Germany, 104, 110

Bayerisches Staatsinstitut für Hochschulforschung und Hochschulplanung (Bavarian State Institute for Research and Planning in HE), Munich, 58

Berdahl, R. O., 5, 10, 17, 22

Boateng, F., 89, 89

Bologna Declaration, 2, 7, 55–57, 59, 64–65, 73, 76–77, 79, 103, 104, 108

Boyer, E., 20, 22, 106, 111

Brazil, 1, 2, 91–98, 102, 104, 105

Brazilian Engineering Teaching Association, 97

Brennan, J., 51

British Columbia, Canada, 24, 27

British North America Act (Canadian constitution), 23

Bruneau, W., 27, 31

Buchbinder, H., 6, 10

Bundesassistentenkonferenz, 61, 62

Cameron, D. M., 26, 31

Campus Compact, 20

Canada, 1, 2, 7, 23–30, 53, 102, 106–107, 110

Canadian Association of University Business Officers, 24, 31

Canadian Association of University Teachers, 23, 24–25, 30, 31

Canadian Society for the Study of Higher Education (CSSHE), 29, 31

CAPES/MEC, 98

Carnegie Academy for the Scholarship of Teaching and Learning (CASTL), 21, 106, 110

Back Issue/Subscription Order Form

Copy or detach and send to:

Jossey-Bass, A Wiley Imprint, 989 Market Street, San Francisco CA 94103-1741
Call or fax toll-free: Phone 888-378-2537 6:30AM–3PM PST; Fax 888-481-2665

Back Issues: Please send me the following issues at $29 each.

                   (Important: please include series initials and issue number, such as HE114.)

_____

_____

_____

$ _____ Total for single issues

$ _____ Shipping charges:

	Surface	Domestic	Canadian
First item		$5.00	$6.00
Each add'l item		$3.00	$1.50

For next-day and second-day delivery rates, call the number listed above.

Subscriptions: Please ___ start ___ renew my subscription to *New Directions for Higher Education* for the year 2_____ at the following rate:

U.S.	___ Individual $80	___ Institutional $180
Canada	___ Individual $80	___ Institutional $220
All others	___ Individual $104	___ Institutional $254

Online subscriptions are available via Wiley InterScience!

For more information about online subscriptions visit
www.wileyinterscience.com

$_____ Total single issues and subscriptions (Add appropriate sales tax for your state for single issue orders. No sales tax for U.S. subscriptions. Canadian residents, add GST for subscriptions and single issues.)

___ Payment enclosed (U.S. check or money order only)

___ VISA ___ MC ___ AmEx # _____ Exp. date _____

Signature _____ Day phone _____

___ Bill me (U.S. institutional orders only. Purchase order required.)

Purchase order # _____

              Federal Tax ID13559302   **GST 89102 8052**

Name _____

Address _____

_____

Phone _____ E-mail _____

For more information about Jossey-Bass, visit our Web site at www.josseybass.com

OTHER TITLES AVAILABLE IN THE
NEW DIRECTIONS FOR HIGHER EDUCATION SERIES
Martin Kramer, Editor-in-Chief

NEW DIRECTIONS FOR HIGHER EDUCATION IS NOW AVAILABLE ONLINE AT WILEY INTERSCIENCE

What is Wiley InterScience?

Wiley InterScience is the dynamic online content service from John Wiley & Sons delivering the full text of over 300 leading scientific, technical, medical, and professional journals, plus major reference works, the acclaimed *Current Protocols* laboratory manuals, and even the full text of select Wiley print books online.

What are some special features of Wiley InterScience?

Wiley InterScience Alerts is a service that delivers table of contents via e-mail for any journal available on Wiley InterScience as soon as a new issue is published online.
Early View is Wiley's exclusive service presenting individual articles online as soon as they are ready, even before the release of the compiled print issue. These articles are complete, peer-reviewed, and citable.
CrossRef is the innovative multi-publisher reference linking system enabling readers to move seamlessly from a reference in a journal article to the cited publication, typically located on a different server and published by a different publisher.

How can I access Wiley InterScience?

Visit http://www.interscience.wiley.com

Guest Users can browse Wiley InterScience for unrestricted access to journal Tables of Contents and Article Abstracts, or use the powerful search engine.
Registered Users are provided with a *Personal Home Page* to store and manage customized alerts, searches, and links to favorite journals and articles. Additionally, Registered Users can view free Online Sample Issues and preview selected material from major reference works.
Licensed Customers are entitled to access full-text journal articles in PDF, with select journals also offering full-text HTML.

How do I become an Authorized User?

Authorized Users are individuals authorized by a paying Customer to have access to the journals in Wiley InterScience. For example, a university that subscribes to Wiley journals is considered to be the Customer. Faculty, staff and students authorized by the university to have access to those journals in Wiley InterScience are Authorized Users. Users should contact their Library for information on which Wiley journals they have access to in Wiley InterScience.

ASK YOUR INSTITUTION ABOUT WILEY INTERSCIENCE TODAY!